Rise Above: Conquering Fear, Doubt, and Life's Storms

Welcome Message

Welcome to this transformative journey of personal growth and spiritual renewal. I'm so excited to join you on this path, where together we will explore the power of resilience, faith, and courage. This book is designed to help you overcome life's challenges, face transitions with confidence, and deepen your connection with God's purpose for your life.

Whether you are stepping into a new season, navigating a difficult transition, or simply seeking a deeper understanding of yourself and God's plan, this book will empower you with tools to strengthen your faith, embrace change, and build resilience in the face of adversity. Through encouraging messages, practical wisdom, and thought-provoking journal prompts, you'll be inspired to grow in confidence, trust, and purpose.

As we journey through each chapter, my hope is that you will discover the strength that lies within you—strength that comes from God's love, grace, and unwavering presence in your life. Let's begin this journey together, trusting that every step brings us closer to living out our highest potential in Christ.

Prelude

Life is a series of seasons—some full of joy, others full of hardship. But through each season, one truth remains: God is with us, guiding us through every step, offering His strength, peace, and wisdom. This book is for anyone seeking to deepen their faith, build resilience, and navigate life's transitions with confidence and grace.

In a world where change is constant and challenges often feel overwhelming, we can sometimes find ourselves lost in fear, doubt, and uncertainty. This book aims to bring you back to the core of who you are—God's beloved child, equipped with the courage, strength, and grace to rise above life's obstacles. Each chapter addresses key areas of personal growth, such as overcoming fear of failure, embracing change, building resilience, and trusting in God's divine timing. Through practical tools, uplifting affirmations, and thought-provoking journal prompts, you will be encouraged to reflect on your journey, find healing, and step into a life of purpose.

This is not just a journey of self-improvement, but a spiritual awakening—a call to lean into your faith, trust in God's promises, and believe that you are capable of more than you ever imagined. As we walk through these lessons together, my hope is that you will emerge stronger, more confident, and deeply rooted in your identity as a child of God.

Dedication

To my beloved family—my children, grandchildren, great-grandchildren, nieces, nephews, friends, and everyone who has filled my life with love and joy.

Your unwavering support has been my anchor through every challenge and triumph. You have been my foundation, my motivation, and my greatest blessing.

This book is dedicated to each of you, for your love, patience, and encouragement have made all things possible.

I love you all beyond measure.

Table of Contents

Introduction

"Rise Above: Conquering Fear, Doubt, and Life's Storms"

Welcome, dear listener, to this journey of discovery, empowerment, and faith. Whether you're stepping into a new chapter in your career, navigating the unfamiliar waters of a personal loss, or simply seeking deeper meaning in your daily life, I want to remind you that you are not alone. Life is filled with moments of uncertainty, and while we may not always understand why things happen the way they do, there is always a greater purpose waiting for us to uncover.

This book is a guide for those who are ready to move beyond fear and self-doubt, to embrace faith in the face of adversity, and to step boldly into the life they were meant to live. You have been chosen for a reason, and I believe you are stronger and more capable than you might realize right now. Together, we'll walk through these moments of transition and emerge with greater clarity, resilience, and confidence.

So, take a deep breath and open your heart. This is your time.

Chapter 1: The Lies We Tell Ourselves – Breaking Free from Self-Doubt

Speak: *Empowering and bold tone, with empathy*

We all hear that voice inside—*the one that whispers lies into our minds, convincing us that we're not good enough, not smart enough, not strong enough.* But let me tell you something, and I want you to hear this clearly: **You are enough**.

That voice of doubt, that fear of failure—it's not your truth. It's a barrier, an illusion, built over time by fear, past experiences, and comparisons to others. But here's the good news: you have the power to silence that voice. You have the power to reframe the narrative in your mind.

You see, self-doubt is often born out of the stories we've internalized. Maybe someone told you as a child that you wouldn't amount to much. Maybe you faced rejection that made you question your worth. But what if I told you that every setback you've faced has been setting you up for something greater? What if the very thing that made you doubt yourself was simply a part of the journey to discovering your strength?

You were created with purpose. No mistake, no failure, no rejection can ever take that away from you. You are stronger than your fears and bigger than your doubts. It's time to step forward in faith and courage, trusting that the path ahead, while uncertain, is filled with possibility.

Self-doubt is a thief. It robs us of the confidence we need to step into our purpose. But the moment we recognize that those doubts are not truth, we can reclaim our power. You are not the lies you've been told, nor the limitations you've placed on yourself. You are more capable, more deserving, and more equipped than you realize.

Now, it's time to break free from those lies. Every time self-doubt creeps in, remind yourself of this truth: *God did not create you to live small.* He has a plan for your life that goes beyond what you can see right now, and your doubts are simply stepping stones to realizing your strength.

Affirmations for Overcoming Self-Doubt:

1. I am enough just as I am, and I am worthy of all the good things life has to offer.

2. My past does not define me; my potential is limitless.

3. I choose faith over fear, and I trust in the path ahead of me.

4. I release the lies that hold me back, and I step into my purpose with confidence.

Reflections - Exercise #1:

1. How can I replace self-doubt with faith and trust in the process?

2. What is one small, brave step I can take today to move past my doubts?

3. In what areas of my life have I already overcome
   doubts? How can I celebrate that growth?

4. Who has God created me to be, and how can I
   honor that vision by stepping out of fear?

Chapter 2: Faith Through the Storm – Finding Strength in Difficult Times

Speak: *Faith-centered and compassionate tone*

Difficult times will come. There will be moments when the weight of life feels too heavy to bear. Loss, disappointment, and pain have a way of shaking us to our core. And it's in those moments that our faith becomes our anchor.

If you're going through a storm right now, I want to acknowledge that pain. *It's real, and it's heavy.* But I also want to remind you that even in the darkest of times, there is a light that never fades—*the light of your faith*. When you feel weak, lean into that light. God's strength is made perfect in our weakness, and when you can't carry the load, remember that He is carrying you.

There is a passage in 2 Corinthians 12:9 that says, "My grace is sufficient for you, for my power is made perfect in weakness." This is your reminder that you don't have to have it all together. You don't have to be strong all the time. It's okay to feel weak, to cry, to wonder. But never lose sight of your faith, because it's that faith that will carry you through to the other side.

The storm may be raging now, but know this: **it will pass**. And when it does, you will emerge stronger, wiser, and with a deeper sense of purpose. Hold on, my friend. The best is yet to come.

Life's storms can feel overwhelming, but it's during these times that your faith becomes your greatest ally. When the winds of doubt, fear, and pain blow hard, remember that you are anchored in something greater than the storm—*you are anchored in faith*. God's grace is a constant, no matter how turbulent life gets. He has promised to never leave you, and that promise remains even when you can't see a way forward.

The challenges you face are not meant to destroy you, but to shape you into the person you are destined to become. The storm may be raging now, but after every storm, the sky clears, and a new day begins. Your new day is coming, and with it, a stronger, more resilient version of you.

Affirmations for Strength in Difficult Times:

1. I am not alone in this storm; my faith is my anchor.

2. God's grace is sufficient for me, even when I feel weak.

3. This season is temporary, and I will emerge stronger and wiser.

4. I trust that everything I am going through is preparing me for something greater.

5. I lean into my faith, knowing that God's plan for me is good, even when I don't understand it.

Reflections - Exercise #2:

1. What is the hardest part of the storm I'm facing right now, and how can I lean into my faith for strength?

2. How has God already shown up for me in previous storms?

3. What is one area where I need to surrender my worries and trust God's plan?

4. How can I use this time of difficulty to grow closer
   to God and build my faith?

5. What lessons might God be teaching me through
   this challenge, and how can I embrace them?

Chapter 3: Building Confidence – Reclaiming Your Power

Speak: Confident and empowering tone

Confidence isn't about always feeling sure of yourself. It's about choosing to move forward even when you feel uncertain. It's about believing in your worth, your abilities, and your purpose, despite what the world may tell you.

The world will try to strip you of your confidence. Whether it's through setbacks, criticism, or the relentless pressures of comparison, the world will try to make you feel less than. But here's what you need to know: **Confidence doesn't come from the world—it comes from within.** It comes from knowing that your worth isn't tied to your achievements or what others think of you. Your worth is inherent, given to you by the Creator Himself.

To build confidence, you need to trust the process. Every small step forward matters. Celebrate your progress, no matter how small. Confidence is built one decision at a time, one risk at a time, and one bold move at a time.

Confidence isn't arrogance, nor is it about perfection. It's about knowing your worth, standing in your truth, and understanding that God has equipped you with everything you need to succeed. Building confidence is a journey, one that requires you to show up for yourself, even when it feels uncomfortable.

The world will try to make you feel small. It will tell you that you're not enough or that you need to fit into a mold. But true confidence comes when you reject those lies and step into the truth of who you are. You are uniquely made, and there is no one else who can fulfill the purpose you've been given. So walk boldly, knowing that your confidence is rooted in the One who created you.

Affirmations for Building Confidence:

1. I am fearfully and wonderfully made, and I walk confidently in my purpose.

2. I release the need for perfection and embrace my unique journey.

3. I am equipped, capable, and ready to step into my calling.

4. I trust in God's plan for me, and I have the courage to take bold steps forward.

5. My confidence comes from knowing my worth is rooted in who God says I am, not in what the world thinks of me.

Reflections - Exercise #3:

1. In what areas of my life do I lack confidence, and how can I begin to reclaim my power?

2. What lies or comparisons have held me back from feeling confident?

3. How can I remind myself daily that my worth is not tied to external validation?

4. What is one bold action I can take this week to build my confidence?

5. How has God equipped me for this season, and how can I show up for myself with boldness?

Chapter 4: Navigating Change with Grace – Finding Resilience in Life's Transitions

Speak: Empathetic and bold tone

Change is inevitable, and yet, it's something most of us resist. We like the comfort of the familiar, but life doesn't allow us to stay in one place for too long. Whether it's a new career path, a loss, or a shift in your personal life, change can feel disorienting, even overwhelming.

But here's something to remember: **Change is not your enemy.** It's an invitation. An invitation to grow, to evolve, and to become the person you were always meant to be. Resilience isn't about avoiding change—it's about learning to dance through it with grace and faith.

In Ecclesiastes 3:1, we are reminded, "To everything, there is a season, and a time for every purpose under the heaven." Your season may be shifting, but it's part of a divine plan. Trust that with every change, you are being guided toward something greater. Embrace it, and don't be afraid to let go of what no longer serves you. You are being prepared for your next chapter.

Change is never easy, but it's often necessary for growth. Every new chapter brings new opportunities to learn, to evolve, and to strengthen your faith. Change isn't something to fear, but something to embrace. It's a sign that you are moving forward, that you are growing into the person God designed you to be.

Resilience doesn't mean avoiding challenges; it means facing them head-on with grace and faith, knowing that God is with you in every transition. When life shifts unexpectedly, remind yourself that **change is part of your journey**. It may feel uncomfortable, but you are being prepared for something greater. With each step forward, you are becoming more resilient, more grounded in faith, and more connected to your purpose.

Affirmations for Resilience in Life's Transitions:

1. I embrace change as a part of my growth and trust God's plan for my life.

2. I am resilient, and I rise with grace through every challenge.

3. Change is a doorway to new possibilities, and I step forward with faith.

4. I release fear and embrace the new season God is guiding me into.

5. I trust that God is using every transition to shape me into the person I am meant to become.

Reflections - Exercise #4:

1. What changes in my life am I resisting, and how can I approach them with grace and faith?

2. How have I shown resilience in the past, and how can I draw strength from those experiences now?

3. What opportunities might be hidden in the changes I'm experiencing?

4. How can I lean on God and trust His guidance during this transition?

5. What new possibilities is God opening up for me through this change, and how can I step forward in faith?

Chapter 5: Stepping Into Your Calling – Discovering Purpose Beyond Fear

Speak: Empowering and bold tone, with a spiritual foundation

Introduction:

Fear has a way of keeping us small. It tells us that we're not capable, not ready, not worthy. But the truth is, God never intended for us to live a life confined by fear. He has called each of us to a unique purpose—one that only we can fulfill. Stepping into that calling can be intimidating, but it's also the most liberating decision you'll ever make.

In this chapter, we will explore what it means to step into your calling. We will identify the fears that hold you back, uncover the God-given purpose within you, and provide actionable steps to move forward with faith, confidence, and clarity. By the end, you'll see that living in your calling is not only possible, but it's what you were designed to do.

Understanding Your Calling:

When we talk about "calling," we often think of a grand, life-changing mission, something that will impact the world on a massive scale. But the truth is, your calling doesn't always start with a big, dramatic revelation. Often, it begins with a small whisper—an inner nudge toward something meaningful. It may be a desire you've carried in your heart for years, or perhaps it's a new curiosity that's recently emerged.

Your calling isn't necessarily tied to a specific career or job title. Instead, it's the thing that brings you alive, the passion that drives you to create, serve, or contribute in a way that feels purposeful. It's what makes you feel connected to something greater than yourself. For some, this calling might be raising a family, serving their community, or creating art. For others, it might be building a business, writing a book, or mentoring young people.

No matter how your calling manifests, it is uniquely yours. You were created with specific gifts, talents, and passions that are designed to be used in this world. Ephesians 2:10 tells us, "For we are God's handiwork, created in Christ Jesus to do good works, which God prepared in advance for us to do." This scripture reminds us that our purpose is not an accident; it was carefully crafted by God before we even entered the world.

So, how do you begin to recognize your calling? One way is to look at the desires of your heart. Psalm 37:4 says, "Take delight in the Lord, and He will give you the desires of your heart." This isn't about God granting us every wish or want, but about Him placing deep desires in our hearts that align with His will. When you delight in God, your heart becomes attuned to His purpose for you. What are the passions and dreams that won't leave you? What stirs your soul and makes you feel most alive?

Facing Fear and Doubt:
One of the biggest obstacles to stepping into your calling is fear. Fear of failure, fear of judgment, fear of the unknown. These fears can feel overwhelming, and they often cause us to stay in our comfort zones rather than take a risk. But here's the truth: fear is normal. Even the most successful, purpose-driven people experience fear.

Consider the story of Moses. When God called Moses to lead the Israelites out of Egypt, Moses didn't immediately jump at the opportunity. In fact, he resisted. He doubted his abilities, questioned why God would choose him, and even begged God to send someone else. Moses said, "Who am I that I should go to Pharaoh and bring the Israelites out of Egypt?" (Exodus 3:11). He was consumed with fear and self-doubt, just like many of us when we feel called to something bigger than ourselves.

But God didn't let Moses off the hook. Instead, He reassured Moses that He would be with him every step of the way. God didn't call Moses because he was perfect; He called him because He had a plan for him. And the same is true for you. God doesn't call the qualified—He qualifies the called.

When fear creeps in, remember that your calling is not about you—it's about the purpose God wants to fulfill through you. Your fear is not an indication that you're on the wrong path; it's simply a reminder that you're about to step into something bigger than yourself. And that's where faith comes in. Faith is the bridge that takes you from fear to action.

Practical Steps to Overcome Fear and Step Into Your Calling:
Now that we've identified fear as a natural part of the process, let's talk about how to move beyond it. Here are some practical steps to help you overcome fear and begin living in your calling:

1. **Acknowledge Your Fear:**
   The first step to overcoming fear is acknowledging it. Don't ignore or suppress your fear; instead, face it head-on. Write down the fears that are holding you back. Are you afraid of failure? Rejection? Uncertainty? By naming your fears, you take away some of their power.

2. **Pray for Strength and Guidance:**
   God wants to partner with you in your purpose. Bring your fears to Him in prayer and ask for the strength to move forward. Isaiah 41:10 reminds us, "So do not fear, for I am with you; do not be dismayed, for I am your God. I will strengthen you and help you; I will uphold you with my righteous right hand." Trust that God will guide you through the challenges.

3. **Take Small Steps of Faith:**
   You don't have to make a huge leap all at once. Start small. Take one step toward your calling today, whether that's researching, reaching out to a mentor, or setting aside time for reflection. Each small step builds momentum and confidence.

4. **Surround Yourself with Supportive People:**
   Surround yourself with people who believe in you and your calling. Share your fears and dreams with trusted friends, family, or mentors. Their encouragement can help you stay focused on your purpose when fear tries to pull you back.

5. **Remember Who You Are in Christ:**
   Your identity is rooted in Christ, not in your performance or achievements. You are loved, chosen, and equipped for this calling. Romans 8:31 tells us, "If God is for us, who can be against us?" When you remember that God is on your side, fear loses its grip.

Your Calling is Unique:

One of the most dangerous things you can do when stepping into your calling is to compare yourself to others. Comparison breeds insecurity and dissatisfaction. But your calling was never meant to look like someone else's. What God has for you is for you.

In the parable of the talents (Matthew 25:14-30), we learn about three servants who were entrusted with different amounts of talents (money) by their master. The master expected them to invest and grow what they were given. Two of the servants doubled their talents and were rewarded. However, the third servant, out of fear, buried his talent in the ground and did nothing with it.

This parable teaches us an important lesson: it's not about how much you've been given, but what you do with what you've been entrusted. Don't waste time comparing your gifts to someone else's. Instead, focus on developing the unique talents and opportunities God has placed in your hands.

God doesn't need you to be anyone other than who He created you to be. Your calling is yours for a reason. The world needs your voice, your perspective, and your gifts. When you step into your calling, you not only honor God, but you also bless those around you by fulfilling your role in His greater plan.

The Cost of Not Pursuing Your Calling:
Stepping into your calling requires courage, faith, and persistence. It's not always easy, but the cost of not pursuing your calling is far greater. When you ignore your calling, you deny the world the gift that only you can bring. You miss out on the joy and fulfillment that comes from living with purpose.

But even more than that, you miss out on the opportunity to partner with God in His work. God is always at work in the world, and He invites us to join Him in that work. When we say "yes" to our calling, we are saying "yes" to being part of something bigger than ourselves.

Think about it this way: your calling is not just about you. It's about the lives you'll impact, the people you'll serve, and the difference you'll make. When you choose to step into your calling, you give others permission to do the same. You become a light, a source of inspiration, and a testimony of God's faithfulness.

Closing Thoughts:

Stepping into your calling is one of the most courageous things you'll ever do. It requires faith, persistence, and a willingness to face your fears head-on. But the rewards are immeasurable. When you align your life with God's purpose, you experience a sense of fulfillment that nothing else can provide.

Remember, you don't have to have it all figured out today. Your calling will continue to unfold as you take steps of faith. Trust the process, trust yourself, and most importantly, trust God. He is with you every step of the way.

Your calling is waiting for you. Will you step into it?

Affirmations for Discovering Purpose:

1. I am created with a unique purpose that only I can fulfill, and I trust that God is guiding me toward my true calling.

2. I release fear and step boldly into my purpose.

3. I am equipped with the gifts needed to make a difference in the world.

4. My purpose is unfolding perfectly in God's timing.

Reflections - Exercise #5:

1. What dreams or passions has God placed on my heart, and how can I begin to explore them?

2. How has fear held me back from stepping into my purpose?

3. What gifts do I possess that I can use to serve others?

4. How can I take one step toward living out my calling today?

Chapter 6: The Power of Gratitude – Shifting Your Focus to Abundance

Speak: Compassionate and uplifting tone, encouraging a mindset shift

Introduction:
Gratitude is often one of the most underestimated yet powerful practices we can incorporate into our daily lives. It has the ability to transform our perspective, reshape our circumstances, and open our hearts to receive abundance in ways we never imagined. But gratitude isn't just about saying "thank you" for the good things. It's a mindset, a lifestyle, and a spiritual discipline that allows us to see God's hand in every moment—whether joyful or challenging.

In this chapter, we'll dive into the life-changing power of gratitude. We'll explore how a grateful heart shifts us from a mindset of lack and scarcity to one of abundance and fullness. You'll discover that when you focus on the blessings in your life, no matter how small, you unlock doors to even greater blessings. Gratitude doesn't just change how you feel—it changes how you experience the world around you.

Understanding Gratitude as a Spiritual Practice:
Gratitude is much more than a polite gesture; it's a spiritual practice rooted in faith. Throughout the Bible, we are called to give thanks in all circumstances—not just when things are going well, but also in times of difficulty. 1 Thessalonians 5:18 tells us, "Give thanks in all circumstances; for this is God's will for you in Christ Jesus." Notice that the scripture doesn't say to give thanks *for* all circumstances, but *in* all circumstances.

This distinction is important because it means we can find something to be grateful for even when life feels hard or overwhelming. Gratitude allows us to look beyond our immediate struggles and recognize that God is still at work in our lives. It shifts our focus from what's missing to what's already present. Even in seasons of waiting, pain, or uncertainty, there is always something to be thankful for.

Think about it: every breath you take, every sunrise you witness, every small act of kindness you experience is a gift. Gratitude teaches us to stop, notice, and appreciate these everyday miracles that we often take for granted.

When you practice gratitude consistently, you begin to realize that abundance isn't just about material wealth or external success. True abundance comes from recognizing the fullness of life that God has already given you. It's found in the love of family and friends, in the beauty of nature, and in the quiet moments of peace. Gratitude helps us see that we are already rich in the things that matter most.

Gratitude in Times of Struggle:
It's easy to be grateful when things are going well, but what about when life takes an unexpected turn? How do we find gratitude when we're facing loss, disappointment, or uncertainty? The truth is, gratitude is not about denying or minimizing the difficulties we face. Instead, it's about choosing to see the blessings that still exist even in the midst of hardship.

Take the story of Job, for example. Job was a man who lost everything—his wealth, his health, his family. Yet, in the midst of his suffering, Job remained faithful and continued to praise God. "The Lord gave and the Lord has taken away; may the name of the Lord be praised" (Job 1:21). Job's ability to remain grateful, even in his darkest hour, is a powerful example of what it means to trust God and give thanks, not for the circumstances, but for the presence of God in the midst of them.

Gratitude during times of struggle doesn't come naturally—it's a choice we make. It requires us to look beyond our immediate situation and trust that God is still working, even when we can't see it. Romans 8:28 reminds us that "in all things God works for the good of those who love him, who have been called according to his purpose." Gratitude helps us hold onto this truth and stay anchored in faith, even when life feels uncertain.

When you practice gratitude in the face of hardship, you are making a bold declaration of faith. You are choosing to believe that God is good, that He is for you, and that His plans for you are still unfolding, even when the path is unclear. Gratitude shifts your focus from what you've lost to what you still have—and that shift has the power to transform your outlook on life.

The Ripple Effect of Gratitude:
Gratitude doesn't just change you; it changes the people around you. When you live from a place of thankfulness, you naturally spread that positivity to others. Think about how you feel when someone expresses genuine gratitude toward you. It lifts your spirit, strengthens your connection, and inspires you to do the same for others.

Now imagine what would happen if you made gratitude a daily practice—not just in your thoughts, but in your actions. Expressing gratitude to others can create a ripple effect that transforms relationships, communities, and even workplaces. When you make a habit of saying "thank you" to the people in your life, you're not just acknowledging their kindness—you're reminding them of their value.

Gratitude fosters deeper connections with others because it focuses on what's right rather than what's wrong. In relationships, it's easy to get caught up in frustrations or unmet expectations, but gratitude shifts the focus to appreciation. Instead of complaining about what your spouse or partner didn't do, gratitude helps you appreciate the ways they show love and support. Instead of focusing on what your friends or coworkers lack, gratitude highlights their strengths and contributions.

This shift from criticism to appreciation can heal strained relationships and create an environment where people feel valued and seen. Gratitude has the power to build bridges where there were once walls. Proverbs 16:24 says, "Gracious words are a honeycomb, sweet to the soul and healing to the bones." When you speak words of gratitude, you bring healing not only to others but also to yourself.

Practical Ways to Cultivate Gratitude:
Gratitude is a practice, and like any practice, it requires intentionality. Here are some practical ways to cultivate gratitude in your daily life:

1. **Start a Gratitude Journal:**
   Each day, write down three things you're grateful for. These don't have to be grand or life-changing moments; they can be as simple as a hot cup of coffee in the morning, a kind word from a friend, or a moment of quiet reflection. The act of writing them down helps you focus on the good in your life and makes gratitude a habit.

2. **Practice Gratitude During Prayer:**
   Incorporate gratitude into your daily prayers. Before asking for anything, take a moment to thank God for what He's already done. This shifts

your mindset from "I need" to "I am thankful,"
and it helps you enter a state of trust and peace.

3. **Express Gratitude to Others:**
   Make it a point to thank the people in your life—
   whether it's your spouse, children, coworkers, or
   even a stranger. A simple "thank you" can go a
   long way in brightening someone's day and
   strengthening your connection.

4. **Shift Negative Thoughts to Gratitude:**
   When you catch yourself focusing on what's
   wrong, consciously shift your thoughts to what's
   right. If you're frustrated with a situation at work,
   pause and think about one thing you can be
   grateful for in that moment. This mental shift can
   change your attitude and help you approach
   challenges with a more positive outlook.

5. **Practice Gratitude in the Morning and Evening:**
   Begin and end your day with gratitude. When you
   wake up, thank God for the gift of a new day and
   the opportunities it holds. Before you go to bed,
   reflect on the moments of the day for which
   you're grateful. This bookends your day with a
   spirit of thankfulness and sets the tone for how
   you experience life.

Gratitude as a Path to Abundance:
When you practice gratitude consistently, you begin to
see the world through a lens of abundance. You realize
that you already have everything you need to live a life
of purpose and joy. Gratitude reminds us that
abundance is not about having more; it's about
appreciating what we already have.

The Bible is filled with examples of people who trusted
in God's abundance, even when their circumstances

seemed dire. Consider the story of the feeding of the five thousand in Matthew 14:13-21. Jesus was faced with a crowd of thousands, and all He had was five loaves of bread and two fish. Yet, before multiplying the food, Jesus gave thanks. His gratitude, even in the face of what seemed like insufficiency, opened the door for a miracle.

This story teaches us an important lesson about gratitude and abundance. When we give thanks for what we have, no matter how small it may seem, we invite God's blessing and multiplication. Gratitude is the key that unlocks the door to abundance because it shifts our focus from what we lack to what we have. And when we focus on what we have, we realize that we have more than enough.

The Science Behind Gratitude:
While gratitude is deeply spiritual, it's also backed by science. Research has shown that practicing gratitude can improve mental health, increase happiness, and even enhance physical well-being. Gratitude has been linked to lower levels of stress, reduced symptoms of depression, and improved relationships. When you practice gratitude, your brain releases dopamine and serotonin—two chemicals that promote feelings of happiness and well-being.

In fact, a study from the Greater Good Science Center at the University of California, Berkeley, found that people who kept a gratitude journal experienced significant improvements in their mental health and overall life satisfaction. This is because gratitude helps rewire the brain to focus on positive experiences rather than negative ones. It literally changes how we think and feel.

When you practice gratitude regularly, you train your brain to seek out the good in every situation. Over time, this becomes your default mindset. Instead of dwelling on what's missing, you begin to see the blessings all around you—and that shift has a profound impact on your emotional and spiritual well-being.

Conclusion:

Gratitude is more than a feel-good practice; it's a transformative mindset that invites abundance, healing, and deeper connection with God and others. When you choose to focus on the blessings in your life, you open the door for more goodness to flow in. Gratitude reminds us that we are already rich in the things that matter most.

As you cultivate a heart of gratitude, you will begin to see your life in a new light. The challenges won't disappear, but your ability to navigate them with grace and faith will grow. You'll realize that abundance is not about having everything you want—it's about appreciating everything you have.

So today, choose gratitude. Choose to see the blessings, big and small, and trust that God is working for your good in every moment.

Affirmations for Gratitude:

1. I am grateful for all that I have and all that is coming to me.

2. My heart is filled with gratitude for the blessings in my life.

3. I choose to focus on abundance and appreciate the small miracles around me.

4. Gratitude opens the door to more blessings; I trust that everything in my life is unfolding for my highest good.

Reflections - Exercise #6:

1. What are three things I am deeply grateful for today?

2. How has focusing on lack affected my mindset, and how can I shift that to abundance?

3. How can I make gratitude a daily practice?

4. How can gratitude help me see difficult situations from a different perspective?

Chapter 7: The Art of Letting Go – Releasing What No Longer Serves You

Speak: Compassionate and uplifting tone, encouraging a mindset shift

Introduction:

Letting go is one of the most powerful acts of faith and healing. Yet, it's also one of the hardest things to do. We hold on to what's familiar, even when it no longer serves us, because the unknown feels too uncertain, too uncomfortable. But clinging to the past, whether it's a hurt, a relationship, or a fear, keeps us stuck in places where we can't grow. Letting go is not about giving up—it's about releasing what is no longer aligned with the person you are becoming so that you can make space for new blessings and opportunities.

In this chapter, we will explore the art of letting go. Together, we'll learn how to identify the things that no longer serve you and how to release them with grace and faith. You'll discover that letting go isn't about losing control—it's about trusting God with the next chapter of your life. By the end, you'll see that the act of letting go is actually an act of love—both for yourself and for the new life that awaits you.

Why We Hold On:

Letting go is difficult, not because we don't want to move forward, but because we are afraid of what will happen if we do. We fear that releasing the familiar will leave us vulnerable or lost. In many cases, holding on feels safer than stepping into the unknown. But the truth is, holding on to something that no longer serves you can be more damaging than letting go. It prevents you from stepping into the fullness of what God has for you.

So why do we hold on? There are several reasons:

1. **Fear of Change:**
   Change is uncomfortable, and letting go often requires stepping into unfamiliar territory. We fear that if we let go of what we know, we'll lose our sense of security. Even if the situation is painful or unfulfilling, it feels predictable. But the problem with holding on to what's comfortable is that it prevents us from growing. God often calls us to new things, but we can't embrace them if we're clinging to the past.

2. **Attachment to Identity:**
   Sometimes, we hold on to things because they've become part of our identity. We might stay in a job or relationship because we've invested so much time and energy into it, and letting go feels like losing a part of ourselves. But your identity is not defined by your circumstances—it is rooted in who you are in Christ. Letting go allows you to evolve and step into new aspects of your true self.

3. **Unresolved Emotions:**
   Holding on can also stem from unresolved emotions like anger, guilt, or regret. Maybe someone hurt you, and you haven't been able to forgive them. Or maybe you feel guilty about a decision you made in the past. These emotions keep us tethered to the past, but they also keep us stuck in a place of pain. Letting go isn't about denying your emotions—it's about healing them and choosing to move forward.

4. **Fear of the Unknown:**
   The unknown can be terrifying. When we let go of something, we often don't know what's on the other side. But here's the truth: God is already on

the other side, waiting for you. He's prepared the next chapter of your life, but you can't walk into it while you're holding on to the last one.

The Spiritual Practice of Letting Go:
Letting go is not just an emotional or mental process—it's a spiritual practice. It requires surrendering your desire for control and trusting that God's plan is greater than anything you could orchestrate on your own. In Matthew 16:24, Jesus says, "Whoever wants to be my disciple must deny themselves and take up their cross and follow me." Part of taking up your cross is letting go of the things that weigh you down, the things that are holding you back from following Him fully.

When we let go, we are making a declaration of trust. We are saying to God, "I trust you with my future more than I trust myself." This act of surrender opens the door to new opportunities, relationships, and experiences that are in alignment with God's will for our lives.

The story of Abraham is a powerful example of the spiritual practice of letting go. In Genesis 12, God called Abraham to leave his home, his family, and everything familiar to go to a land that God would show him. Abraham didn't know where he was going, but he trusted God enough to let go of what he knew. Because of his faith, Abraham became the father of many nations, and God's promise to him was fulfilled.

Like Abraham, we are often called to let go of the familiar so that we can step into the unknown with faith. It's in the letting go that we find the space for God's blessings to unfold in our lives.

Letting Go of Relationships:
One of the most challenging aspects of letting go is

releasing relationships that are no longer serving us. This doesn't always mean ending a relationship, but it might mean redefining boundaries or letting go of unhealthy patterns. Relationships, whether romantic, familial, or friendships, are meant to nurture and support us. When a relationship becomes toxic, one-sided, or harmful, it's important to evaluate whether holding on is truly in your best interest.

In John 15:2, Jesus says, "He cuts off every branch in me that bears no fruit, while every branch that does bear fruit he prunes so that it will be even more fruitful." This verse speaks to the necessity of pruning in our lives. Just as a gardener prunes a plant to encourage new growth, sometimes God removes certain people or situations from our lives to make room for what's next. Holding on to relationships that no longer bear fruit can stunt your growth.

Letting go of a relationship doesn't mean you don't care for the person or that the relationship didn't serve a purpose. It simply means that its season in your life may have come to an end. Trust that God will bring new, healthy relationships into your life that will align with your growth and purpose.

If you're struggling to let go of a relationship, ask yourself these questions:

- Is this relationship bringing out the best in me, or is it draining my energy?

- Am I holding on out of fear of being alone or because I truly believe this relationship is part of God's plan for my life?

- What would it look like to set healthier boundaries in this relationship?

Letting Go of the Past:
The past has a way of holding on to us long after we've left it behind. Whether it's past mistakes, regrets, or missed opportunities, we often carry the weight of what could have been. But living in the past keeps us from fully embracing the present and moving forward into the future God has for us.

Philippians 3:13-14 encourages us to "forget what is behind and strain toward what is ahead, pressing on toward the goal to win the prize for which God has called [us] heavenward in Christ Jesus." Paul's words remind us that we can't run the race God has set before us if we're constantly looking backward. Letting go of the past doesn't mean ignoring it or pretending it didn't happen. It means releasing its hold on you so that you can move forward without carrying the burden of yesterday's mistakes.

One of the most powerful ways to let go of the past is through forgiveness—both of others and of yourself. When we forgive, we release the emotional grip that the past has on us. Forgiveness doesn't mean excusing someone's actions; it means choosing to free yourself from the anger and resentment that bind you to the past. Likewise, forgiving yourself for past mistakes is essential for healing and growth.

Here are some practical steps to let go of the past:

1. **Acknowledge What You're Holding Onto:** Take time to reflect on the past experiences or regrets that are still weighing on you. Write them down. Acknowledging them is the first step to releasing them.

2. **Forgive Yourself and Others:** Whether it's a situation you regret or a person who hurt you, choose to forgive. This doesn't mean you have to forget or condone what

happened, but it does mean you release the emotional hold it has on you.

3. **Create a New Vision for the Future:**
   Letting go of the past allows you to create space for the future. Take time to envision the life you want to create and ask God to guide you as you step into that new chapter.

Letting Go of Control:
One of the most challenging things to let go of is control. We often think that if we can just manage every detail of our lives, we can avoid pain, disappointment, or failure. But the desire for control is an illusion—it's impossible to control everything. Letting go of control is about trusting that God is in charge and that His plan is better than anything we could plan for ourselves.

Proverbs 3:5-6 reminds us to "Trust in the Lord with all your heart and lean not on your own understanding; in all your ways submit to him, and he will make your paths straight." Trusting God with our lives means surrendering our need to control the outcome and believing that He is guiding us on the right path.

Letting go of control is not a sign of weakness; it's a sign of faith. It's acknowledging that while we don't know what the future holds, we trust the One who holds the future.

Practical Steps to Letting Go:
Letting go is a process, and it doesn't happen overnight. Here are some practical steps to help you on your journey:

1. **Reflect on What You're Holding Onto:**
   Take time to reflect on the areas of your life

where you're struggling to let go. Is it a relationship, a past mistake, or a need for control? Identifying what you're holding onto is the first step toward releasing it.

2. **Surrender Through Prayer:**
   Bring your burdens to God in prayer and ask Him to help you let go. Surrendering through prayer is a powerful way to release control and trust God's plan for your life.

3. **Visualize Letting Go:**
   One helpful exercise is to visualize yourself letting go of what's weighing you down. Imagine yourself holding onto a heavy load and then releasing it, trusting that God will take care of it.

4. **Focus on What You're Gaining, Not What You're Losing:**
   Letting go isn't about loss—it's about making space for new blessings. Shift your focus from what you're releasing to what God is preparing for you in the next chapter of your life.

Conclusion:
Letting go is not about giving up; it's about moving forward. It's about trusting that God has something better for you than what you're holding onto. Whether it's a relationship, a past mistake, or a desire for control, letting go creates space for healing, growth, and new beginnings.

As you practice the art of letting go, remember that you are not alone. God is with you every step of the way, guiding you toward a life of freedom, peace, and abundance. Trust Him with your past, your present, and your future, and watch as He unfolds His perfect plan in your life.

Affirmations for Letting Go:

1. I release what no longer serves me and make space for new blessings.

2. I let go of past hurts and choose to heal.

3. I trust that by letting go, I am creating room for God's greater plan.

4. I am free from old patterns that hold me back.

5. Letting go is an act of faith, and I trust the process.

Reflections - Exercise #7:

1. What is one thing I need to let go of to move forward in my life?

2. How has holding on to past hurts or limiting beliefs kept me stuck?

3. What would my life look like if I truly released these burdens?

4. How can I take a small step today to begin letting go?

Chapter 8: Embracing Imperfection – Finding Beauty in Your Journey

Speak: Empathetic and uplifting tone, encouraging self-compassion

Introduction:

We live in a world that glorifies perfection. From social media filters to society's expectations of success, the message we constantly receive is that we must strive to be flawless in every area of our lives. But this pursuit of perfection is exhausting and unattainable. The truth is, no one is perfect—and trying to be leaves us feeling inadequate, ashamed, or stuck in a cycle of self-criticism.

What if I told you that there is beauty in imperfection? That your flaws, mistakes, and struggles are not things to be ashamed of but opportunities for growth, learning, and connection? In this chapter, we'll explore the power of embracing imperfection and why it is an essential part of your personal and spiritual journey. We'll see how God uses our imperfections for His glory and how accepting our humanity can lead to greater joy, peace, and fulfillment.

By the end of this chapter, you'll learn to release the unrealistic expectations you've placed on yourself and embrace the beauty of your imperfect journey.

The Danger of Perfectionism:

Perfectionism is often seen as a positive trait. After all, who doesn't want to do their best and avoid mistakes? But the problem with perfectionism is that it sets an unattainable standard. It demands that we perform without flaw, and when we inevitably fall short, it leaves us feeling like failures.

At its core, perfectionism is rooted in fear—fear of failure, fear of judgment, fear of not being enough. It convinces us that if we can just be perfect, we'll be worthy of love, success, or approval. But perfectionism isn't about excellence; it's about control. It's about trying to control how others perceive us and how we perceive ourselves. The reality is that perfectionism leads to anxiety, procrastination, and burnout because it's an impossible standard to meet.

Brené Brown, a researcher and author on vulnerability and shame, says it best: "Perfectionism is a twenty-ton shield that we lug around, thinking it will protect us, when in fact, it's the thing that's really preventing us from taking flight."

The irony of perfectionism is that it actually hinders our growth. When we're so focused on being perfect, we avoid taking risks, trying new things, or stepping out of our comfort zone. We become paralyzed by the fear of making mistakes, and as a result, we miss out on the very opportunities that lead to growth and success.

God's Grace in Our Imperfections:
As believers, it's important to remember that God never asks us to be perfect. In fact, the Bible is filled with stories of imperfect people who were used mightily by God. Consider King David, who committed adultery and murder, yet was still called "a man after God's own heart" (Acts 13:22). Or Moses, who doubted his ability to lead and made mistakes, yet was chosen to deliver God's people from Egypt. Even the Apostle Paul, who wrote much of the New Testament, called himself "the worst of sinners" (1 Timothy 1:15).

These examples show us that God doesn't require perfection. Instead, He asks for a willing heart. 2 Corinthians 12:9 says, "My grace is sufficient for you, for my power is made perfect in weakness." This verse is a powerful reminder that our imperfections are not obstacles to God's work—they are opportunities for His grace to shine through.

God's grace is what allows us to move forward despite our imperfections. He uses our weaknesses to show His strength and our failures to teach us valuable lessons. When we stop striving for perfection and start relying on God's grace, we find freedom. We realize that our worth isn't tied to how well we perform or how flawless we appear—it's rooted in the fact that we are loved by a perfect God.

The Beauty of Imperfection:
There's a Japanese art form called *kintsugi*, which means "golden joinery." It's the practice of repairing broken pottery with gold, silver, or platinum. Instead of hiding the cracks, *kintsugi* highlights them, turning the once-broken object into something even more beautiful. The philosophy behind this art form is that there is beauty in imperfection and that the broken parts of an object don't diminish its value—they enhance it.

This is how God sees us. Our imperfections, our struggles, and our broken places are not things to be ashamed of. They are part of what makes us unique and beautiful. Just as the cracks in the pottery are filled with gold, our brokenness is filled with God's grace. The beauty of imperfection is that it allows us to experience God's healing and redemption in ways we never could if we were perfect.

When we embrace our imperfections, we allow ourselves to be vulnerable. And vulnerability is what connects us to others. No one can relate to perfection, but everyone can relate to struggle, failure, and growth. When we are honest about our imperfections, we give others permission to be honest about theirs as well. This creates a space for authentic relationships and deeper connections.

The Trap of Comparison:

One of the biggest obstacles to embracing imperfection is comparison. We live in a culture that constantly bombards us with images of perfection—whether it's on social media, in magazines, or in the lives of people around us. It's easy to look at others and think they have it all together, while we feel like we're falling apart. But the truth is, no one's life is perfect. What we see on the outside is often a carefully curated version of reality, not the whole picture.

Comparison not only breeds discontent, but it also robs us of joy. When we compare ourselves to others, we focus on what we lack rather than appreciating what we have. We become blind to our own unique gifts, talents, and experiences because we're too busy trying to measure up to someone else's standard.

Galatians 6:4 encourages us to "pay careful attention to your own work, for then you will get the satisfaction of a job well done, and you won't need to compare yourself to anyone else." This verse reminds us to focus on our own journey rather than comparing it to someone else's. God has given each of us a unique path, and we can't walk it if we're constantly looking at what others are doing.

How to Embrace Your Imperfections:

Learning to embrace imperfection is a journey, but it's one that leads to greater peace and fulfillment. Here are some practical steps you can take to start embracing your imperfections:

1. **Acknowledge Your Humanity:**
   The first step to embracing imperfection is acknowledging that you are human. You will make mistakes, you will have flaws, and that's okay. Accepting your humanity means giving yourself permission to be less than perfect. You don't have to have it all figured out.

2. **Practice Self-Compassion:**
   Be kind to yourself when you fall short of your expectations. Instead of beating yourself up for not being perfect, treat yourself with the same compassion you would offer a friend. Remember that you are doing your best, and that's enough.

3. **Celebrate Your Progress:**
   Perfectionism often causes us to focus on what we haven't achieved rather than celebrating how far we've come. Take time to acknowledge the progress you've made, no matter how small. Every step forward is worth celebrating.

4. **Let Go of the Need for Approval:**
   One of the reasons we strive for perfection is because we want others to approve of us. But the truth is, you can't please everyone, and trying to do so will only leave you feeling exhausted. Let go of the need for external validation and focus on living authentically.

5. **Trust in God's Plan for Your Life:**
   When we try to control everything and strive for perfection, we're often operating from a place of fear rather than faith. Trust that God's plan for your life is unfolding exactly as it should, imperfections and all. His timing is perfect, even when yours is not.

The Freedom in Letting Go of Perfection:
When you embrace your imperfections, you experience a freedom that perfectionism can never provide. You no longer have to carry the weight of unrealistic expectations or the constant pressure to perform. Instead, you can rest in the knowledge that you are enough just as you are.

This freedom allows you to live more fully and authentically. You can take risks without the fear of failure holding you back. You can pursue your dreams, knowing that mistakes are part of the journey. You can be vulnerable with others, knowing that your imperfections are what make you relatable and real.

In Matthew 11:28-30, Jesus invites us to come to Him and find rest: "Come to me, all you who are weary and burdened, and I will give you rest. Take my yoke upon you and learn from me, for I am gentle and humble in heart, and you will find rest for your souls." Perfectionism is a burden, but Jesus offers us rest. He reminds us that we don't have to carry the weight of trying to be perfect. We can lay that burden down and find peace in Him.

Perfection Isn't the Goal—Growth Is:
At the end of the day, perfection isn't the goal—growth is. God isn't looking for you to be flawless; He's looking for you to be faithful. When you embrace your imperfections, you open yourself up to growth, learning, and transformation. Each mistake you make is an opportunity to learn something new. Each failure is a stepping stone toward success.

Remember that life is a journey, not a destination. It's not about arriving at a place of perfection; it's about growing into the person God created you to be. And that growth happens in the messy, imperfect moments of life.

Conclusion:

Embracing imperfection is an act of self-compassion, faith, and trust. It's recognizing that you are enough, not because of what you do, but because of who you are in Christ. Your worth is not defined by your ability to be perfect—it's defined by the love of a perfect God.

As you move forward, remember that your imperfections are not weaknesses. They are part of what makes you beautifully human, and they are opportunities for God's grace to shine through. So let go of the need to be perfect, embrace the beauty of your journey, and trust that God is working in and through every imperfect moment.

Affirmations for Embracing Imperfection:

1. I am worthy just as I am, imperfections and all.

2. I release the need for perfection and embrace the beauty of my journey.

3. My mistakes are opportunities for growth and learning.

4. God's grace is sufficient for me, even in my imperfections.

5. I choose to love and accept myself, flaws and all.

Reflections - Exercise #8:

1. In what areas of my life do I struggle with perfectionism?

2. How has striving for perfection held me back from fully enjoying life?

3. What would it feel like to embrace my imperfections and trust that I am enough?

4. How can I show myself more grace and compassion in this season?

Chapter 9: The Power of Forgiveness – Healing Through Grace

Speak: Empathetic and faith-centered tone, focused on healing and renewal

Introduction:

Letting go is one of the most powerful acts of faith and healing. Yet, it's also one of the hardest things to do. We hold on to what's familiar, even when it no longer serves us, because the unknown feels too uncertain, too uncomfortable. But clinging to the past, whether it's a hurt, a relationship, or a fear, keeps us stuck in places where we can't grow. Letting go is not about giving up—it's about releasing what is no longer aligned with the person you are becoming so that you can make space for new blessings and opportunities.

In this chapter, we will explore the art of letting go. Together, we'll learn how to identify the things that no longer serve you and how to release them with grace and faith. You'll discover that letting go isn't about losing control—it's about trusting God with the next chapter of your life. By the end, you'll see that the act of letting go is actually an act of love—both for yourself and for the new life that awaits you.

Why We Hold On:

Letting go is difficult, not because we don't want to move forward, but because we are afraid of what will happen if we do. We fear that releasing the familiar will leave us vulnerable or lost. In many cases, holding on feels safer than stepping into the unknown. But the truth is, holding on to something that no longer serves you can be more damaging than letting go. It prevents you from stepping into the fullness of what God has for you.

So why do we hold on? There are several reasons:

5. **Fear of Change:**
   Change is uncomfortable, and letting go often requires stepping into unfamiliar territory. We fear that if we let go of what we know, we'll lose our sense of security. Even if the situation is painful or unfulfilling, it feels predictable. But the problem with holding on to what's comfortable is that it prevents us from growing. God often calls us to new things, but we can't embrace them if we're clinging to the past.

6. **Attachment to Identity:**
   Sometimes, we hold on to things because they've become part of our identity. We might stay in a job or relationship because we've invested so much time and energy into it, and letting go feels like losing a part of ourselves. But your identity is not defined by your circumstances—it is rooted in who you are in Christ. Letting go allows you to evolve and step into new aspects of your true self.

7. **Unresolved Emotions:**
   Holding on can also stem from unresolved emotions like anger, guilt, or regret. Maybe someone hurt you, and you haven't been able to forgive them. Or maybe you feel guilty about a decision you made in the past. These emotions keep us tethered to the past, but they also keep us stuck in a place of pain. Letting go isn't about denying your emotions—it's about healing them and choosing to move forward.

8. **Fear of the Unknown:**
   The unknown can be terrifying. When we let go of something, we often don't know what's on the other side. But here's the truth: God is already on

the other side, waiting for you. He's prepared the next chapter of your life, but you can't walk into it while you're holding on to the last one.

The Spiritual Practice of Letting Go:

Letting go is not just an emotional or mental process—it's a spiritual practice. It requires surrendering your desire for control and trusting that God's plan is greater than anything you could orchestrate on your own. In Matthew 16:24, Jesus says, "Whoever wants to be my disciple must deny themselves and take up their cross and follow me." Part of taking up your cross is letting go of the things that weigh you down, the things that are holding you back from following Him fully.

When we let go, we are making a declaration of trust. We are saying to God, "I trust you with my future more than I trust myself." This act of surrender opens the door to new opportunities, relationships, and experiences that are in alignment with God's will for our lives.

The story of Abraham is a powerful example of the spiritual practice of letting go. In Genesis 12, God called Abraham to leave his home, his family, and everything familiar to go to a land that God would show him. Abraham didn't know where he was going, but he trusted God enough to let go of what he knew. Because of his faith, Abraham became the father of many nations, and God's promise to him was fulfilled.

Like Abraham, we are often called to let go of the familiar so that we can step into the unknown with faith. It's in the letting go that we find the space for God's blessings to unfold in our lives.

Letting Go of Relationships:

One of the most challenging aspects of letting go is

releasing relationships that are no longer serving us. This doesn't always mean ending a relationship, but it might mean redefining boundaries or letting go of unhealthy patterns. Relationships, whether romantic, familial, or friendships, are meant to nurture and support us. When a relationship becomes toxic, one-sided, or harmful, it's important to evaluate whether holding on is truly in your best interest.

In John 15:2, Jesus says, "He cuts off every branch in me that bears no fruit, while every branch that does bear fruit he prunes so that it will be even more fruitful." This verse speaks to the necessity of pruning in our lives. Just as a gardener prunes a plant to encourage new growth, sometimes God removes certain people or situations from our lives to make room for what's next. Holding on to relationships that no longer bear fruit can stunt your growth.

Letting go of a relationship doesn't mean you don't care for the person or that the relationship didn't serve a purpose. It simply means that its season in your life may have come to an end. Trust that God will bring new, healthy relationships into your life that will align with your growth and purpose.

If you're struggling to let go of a relationship, ask yourself these questions:

- Is this relationship bringing out the best in me, or is it draining my energy?

- Am I holding on out of fear of being alone or because I truly believe this relationship is part of God's plan for my life?

- What would it look like to set healthier boundaries in this relationship?

Letting Go of the Past:
The past has a way of holding on to us long after we've left it behind. Whether it's past mistakes, regrets, or missed opportunities, we often carry the weight of what could have been. But living in the past keeps us from fully embracing the present and moving forward into the future God has for us.

Philippians 3:13-14 encourages us to "forget what is behind and strain toward what is ahead, pressing on toward the goal to win the prize for which God has called [us] heavenward in Christ Jesus." Paul's words remind us that we can't run the race God has set before us if we're constantly looking backward. Letting go of the past doesn't mean ignoring it or pretending it didn't happen. It means releasing its hold on you so that you can move forward without carrying the burden of yesterday's mistakes.

One of the most powerful ways to let go of the past is through forgiveness—both of others and of yourself. When we forgive, we release the emotional grip that the past has on us. Forgiveness doesn't mean excusing someone's actions; it means choosing to free yourself from the anger and resentment that bind you to the past. Likewise, forgiving yourself for past mistakes is essential for healing and growth.

Here are some practical steps to let go of the past:

4. **Acknowledge What You're Holding Onto:**
   Take time to reflect on the past experiences or regrets that are still weighing on you. Write them down. Acknowledging them is the first step to releasing them.

5. **Forgive Yourself and Others:**
   Whether it's a situation you regret or a person who hurt you, choose to forgive. This doesn't mean you have to forget or condone what

happened, but it does mean you release the emotional hold it has on you.

6. **Create a New Vision for the Future:**
   Letting go of the past allows you to create space for the future. Take time to envision the life you want to create and ask God to guide you as you step into that new chapter.

Letting Go of Control:
One of the most challenging things to let go of is control. We often think that if we can just manage every detail of our lives, we can avoid pain, disappointment, or failure. But the desire for control is an illusion—it's impossible to control everything. Letting go of control is about trusting that God is in charge and that His plan is better than anything we could plan for ourselves.

Proverbs 3:5-6 reminds us to "Trust in the Lord with all your heart and lean not on your own understanding; in all your ways submit to him, and he will make your paths straight." Trusting God with our lives means surrendering our need to control the outcome and believing that He is guiding us on the right path.

Letting go of control is not a sign of weakness; it's a sign of faith. It's acknowledging that while we don't know what the future holds, we trust the One who holds the future.

Practical Steps to Letting Go:
Letting go is a process, and it doesn't happen overnight. Here are some practical steps to help you on your journey:

5. **Reflect on What You're Holding Onto:**
   Take time to reflect on the areas of your life

where you're struggling to let go. Is it a relationship, a past mistake, or a need for control? Identifying what you're holding onto is the first step toward releasing it.

6. **Surrender Through Prayer:**
   Bring your burdens to God in prayer and ask Him to help you let go. Surrendering through prayer is a powerful way to release control and trust God's plan for your life.

7. **Visualize Letting Go:**
   One helpful exercise is to visualize yourself letting go of what's weighing you down. Imagine yourself holding onto a heavy load and then releasing it, trusting that God will take care of it.

8. **Focus on What You're Gaining, Not What You're Losing:**
   Letting go isn't about loss—it's about making space for new blessings. Shift your focus from what you're releasing to what God is preparing for you in the next chapter of your life.

Conclusion:

Letting go is not about giving up; it's about moving forward. It's about trusting that God has something better for you than what you're holding onto. Whether it's a relationship, a past mistake, or a desire for control, letting go creates space for healing, growth, and new beginnings.

As you practice the art of letting go, remember that you are not alone. God is with you every step of the way, guiding you toward a life of freedom, peace, and abundance. Trust Him with your past, your present, and your future, and watch as He unfolds His perfect plan in your life.

Affirmations for Forgiveness:

1. I forgive others, not for their sake, but for my own peace.

2. I release bitterness and resentment, choosing healing and grace.

3. Forgiveness is a gift I give to myself. I am no longer defined by the pain of the past.

4. I choose peace, healing, and freedom through forgiveness.

Reflections - Exercise #9:

1. Is there someone I need to forgive to experience healing in my own life?

2. How has holding onto resentment affected my mental, emotional, and spiritual well-being?

3. What would forgiveness look like for me, and how can I begin the process?

4. How can I ask God for the strength and grace to forgive?

____

____

____

____

____

____

Chapter 10: Cultivating Self-Love – Nurturing the Relationship with Yourself

Speak: Compassionate and empowering tone, promoting self-worth

Introduction:
Self-love is often misunderstood in a world that sometimes equates it with selfishness. But true self-love is far from selfish—it's an essential part of living a balanced, joyful, and healthy life. It's about honoring who God created you to be and nurturing the relationship you have with yourself. In many ways, self-love is the foundation for how you relate to others and how you live out your purpose.

Yet, cultivating self-love can be challenging, especially when we've been taught to put others' needs before our own or when we struggle with self-doubt and insecurity. Many of us are far more comfortable giving love to others than accepting it for ourselves. But here's the truth: you cannot pour from an empty cup. If you don't take care of yourself—emotionally, spiritually, and physically—you won't be able to fully show up for others or for the purpose God has placed on your life.

In this chapter, we will explore the importance of self-love, how it aligns with your faith, and how you can begin to nurture the relationship with yourself. By the end, you will see that loving yourself is not only a vital part of your spiritual journey but also a reflection of God's love for you.

Understanding Self-Love as a Spiritual Practice:
At its core, self-love is about recognizing your inherent worth as a child of God. Genesis 1:27 tells us, "So God created mankind in his own image, in the image of God he created them; male and female he created them."

This verse is a powerful reminder that we are created in God's image, and as such, we are worthy of love, care, and respect. When we love ourselves, we honor the One who created us.

Self-love isn't about putting yourself above others or indulging in self-centeredness. Instead, it's about taking care of the body, mind, and spirit that God has entrusted to you. It's about acknowledging that you have value and worth, not because of what you do or how you perform, but simply because you are God's creation.

The Bible also speaks to the importance of loving others as we love ourselves. In Matthew 22:39, Jesus says, "Love your neighbor as yourself." Notice that the command assumes that we love ourselves first. How can we truly love others if we don't extend that same love and compassion to ourselves? Self-love is not separate from the love we show others—it is the foundation for it. When you are kind, compassionate, and loving toward yourself, you are better able to show up as your authentic self in your relationships and in the world.

Why We Struggle with Self-Love:
For many people, self-love doesn't come naturally. We are often our own harshest critics, quick to judge ourselves for our shortcomings while offering grace and kindness to others. But why is it so hard to love ourselves? There are several reasons why we struggle with self-love:

1. **Negative Self-Talk:**
   One of the biggest barriers to self-love is the inner dialogue we have with ourselves. Negative self-talk can be incredibly damaging, and often, we don't even realize we're doing it. Thoughts like

"I'm not good enough," "I'll never succeed," or "I don't deserve love" can become so ingrained in our minds that we begin to believe them. But these thoughts are lies. They are not reflective of who you are in God's eyes.

2. **Unrealistic Expectations:**
We live in a society that sets unrealistic standards for beauty, success, and happiness. Whether it's through social media, advertising, or cultural norms, we are constantly bombarded with messages that tell us we need to be more—more attractive, more successful, more accomplished—to be worthy of love. These unrealistic expectations can lead to feelings of inadequacy and self-doubt.

3. **Past Hurts and Trauma:**
Many of us carry wounds from the past that affect how we view ourselves. Whether it's childhood trauma, failed relationships, or past mistakes, these experiences can create a sense of unworthiness or shame. But holding onto these hurts keeps us stuck in a place of pain. Healing is possible, but it requires self-compassion and the willingness to release the past.

4. **Fear of Judgment:**
Often, we fear that if we truly embrace self-love, others will view us as selfish or self-centered. But self-love is not about seeking approval from others; it's about taking care of your own well-being so that you can live a fuller, more meaningful life. When we base our worth on how others perceive us, we lose sight of our true value.

5. **Spiritual Misdirection:**
Sometimes, we mistakenly believe that focusing

on ourselves goes against our faith. We think that loving others means neglecting our own needs. But this couldn't be further from the truth. Jesus cared for others deeply, but He also took time to rest, pray, and nurture His own relationship with God. If even Jesus, in His humanity, needed time to care for Himself, how much more do we?

The Biblical Foundation for Self-Love:
Self-love is not only important for our mental and emotional well-being—it's a spiritual practice rooted in the teachings of the Bible. God calls us to take care of ourselves and to recognize our worth in Him. Here are some key scriptures that speak to the importance of self-love:

- **Psalm 139:14:** "I praise you because I am fearfully and wonderfully made; your works are wonderful, I know that full well."
  This verse reminds us that we are made in God's image, and everything He creates is good. When you love yourself, you are acknowledging the beauty and worth that God has placed within you.

- **1 Corinthians 6:19-20:** "Do you not know that your bodies are temples of the Holy Spirit, who is in you, whom you have received from God? You are not your own; you were bought at a price. Therefore honor God with your bodies."
  This scripture emphasizes the importance of caring for our physical and spiritual well-being. When you nurture your body, mind, and spirit, you are honoring God.

- **Matthew 11:28:** "Come to me, all you who are weary and burdened, and I will give you rest."
  Jesus invites us to rest in Him. Self-love includes recognizing when you need to rest, rejuvenate,

and care for your own needs so that you can continue to serve and live in alignment with God's purpose.

Practical Ways to Cultivate Self-Love:
Learning to love yourself is a journey, and it's one that requires intentionality. Here are some practical steps to help you cultivate self-love:

1. **Challenge Negative Self-Talk:**
   The way you talk to yourself matters. If you find yourself engaging in negative self-talk, pause and ask yourself, "Would I say this to a friend?" If the answer is no, then it's time to reframe those thoughts. Replace self-criticism with self-compassion. For example, instead of saying, "I'm not good enough," try saying, "I am doing my best, and that is enough."

2. **Set Healthy Boundaries:**
   Self-love includes setting boundaries that protect your mental, emotional, and spiritual health. This might mean saying no to commitments that overwhelm you, distancing yourself from toxic relationships, or taking time for yourself without guilt. Remember, you have the right to prioritize your well-being.

3. **Practice Self-Care:**
   Self-care is an essential part of self-love. It's not just about pampering yourself, but about nourishing your body, mind, and spirit. This can include getting enough sleep, eating nourishing foods, spending time in prayer or meditation, engaging in hobbies you enjoy, and exercising regularly. Self-care is an act of self-love that fuels your ability to show up fully in life.

4. **Forgive Yourself:**
   Just as you extend grace to others, it's important
   to extend grace to yourself. We all make
   mistakes, and holding onto guilt or shame only
   prevents you from moving forward. Forgive
   yourself for past mistakes, and trust that God's
   grace is greater than any of your shortcomings.

5. **Celebrate Your Achievements:**
   Take time to acknowledge your accomplishments,
   no matter how small. Whether it's completing a
   project, overcoming a challenge, or simply
   making it through a difficult day, celebrate your
   progress. Recognizing your efforts reinforces a
   positive self-image and helps you appreciate your
   own growth.

The Connection Between Self-Love and Self-Worth:

At the heart of self-love is a deep understanding of your
worth. Your worth is not defined by your achievements,
appearance, or the opinions of others. It is rooted in the
fact that you are a child of God, created with purpose,
value, and dignity. When you cultivate self-love, you
are affirming this truth: "I am worthy of love, care, and
respect."

Psalm 8:4-5 says, "What is mankind that you are
mindful of them, human beings that you care for them?
You have made them a little lower than the angels and
crowned them with glory and honor." This scripture
reminds us of the immense value God places on each of
us. If God sees us as worthy of honor and love, we
must learn to see ourselves in the same light.

When you truly understand your worth in God's eyes,
self-love becomes a natural expression of that
understanding. You no longer feel the need to seek

validation from external sources because you are secure in the knowledge that you are already enough. This security allows you to live more authentically, free from the pressure to prove yourself or meet unrealistic standards.

How Self-Love Impacts Relationships:
One of the most beautiful things about self-love is that it enhances your ability to love others. When you are kind, compassionate, and forgiving toward yourself, you are better able to extend those same qualities to others. You no longer rely on others to fill emotional voids because you are already filled with a sense of worth and wholeness.

Self-love also sets the standard for how others treat you. When you love and respect yourself, you communicate that you are deserving of the same love and respect from others. This creates healthier, more balanced relationships. You are less likely to tolerate toxic behavior or settle for less than you deserve because you know your worth.

In Ephesians 5:29, Paul writes, "After all, no one ever hated their own body, but they feed and care for their body, just as Christ does the church." This verse highlights the importance of caring for ourselves so that we can, in turn, care for others. When you love yourself, you create a foundation of emotional and spiritual health that benefits not only you but also those around you.

Overcoming the Fear of Self-Love:
For some, the idea of self-love feels uncomfortable or even selfish. You may fear that focusing on yourself will take away from your ability to serve others or that people will judge you for putting your needs first. But

self-love is not about indulgence or self-centeredness—it's about maintaining the balance that allows you to serve from a place of fullness.

Jesus often took time away from the crowds to pray, rest, and reconnect with God. In Luke 5:16, it says, "But Jesus often withdrew to lonely places and prayed." If Jesus, who was constantly serving others, needed time for Himself, how much more do we? Self-love is not a distraction from your purpose—it's what equips you to fulfill it.

Overcoming the fear of self-love means trusting that caring for yourself is part of God's design for your life. It means recognizing that you are worthy of love, rest, and nourishment, just as much as anyone else. When you release the fear of judgment or guilt, you create space for healing, growth, and greater service to others.

Conclusion:
Self-love is an essential part of your spiritual journey. It's not about vanity or selfishness—it's about honoring the person God created you to be. When you cultivate self-love, you nurture the relationship with yourself, strengthen your relationship with God, and create a foundation for healthier relationships with others.

As you begin to practice self-love, remember that you are worthy, valuable, and deserving of the same love and care that you give to others. By loving yourself, you are reflecting God's love in your life and honoring His creation. Let go of the fear, doubt, and guilt that hold you back, and step into the fullness of who you are.

Affirmations for Self-Love:

1. I love and accept myself just as I am. I honor my body, mind, and spirit with care and compassion.

2. I am worthy of love, joy, and peace.

3. I choose to see myself through God's eyes, as someone valuable and loved.

4. My self-love is a reflection of God's love for me.

Reflections - Exercise #10:

1. In what ways have I neglected my own needs and well-being?

2. How can I begin to nurture a deeper relationship with myself?

3. What negative beliefs do I hold about myself, and how can I begin to release them?

4. How can I show myself more love and compassion in my daily life?

____

____

____

____

____

____

____

Chapter 11: Reclaiming Your Power – Setting Boundaries with Confidence

Speak: Bold and empowering tone, focused on self-respect and confidence

Introduction:

Boundaries are a vital part of a healthy and balanced life. Yet, many of us struggle with setting and maintaining them. We fear being seen as selfish, unkind, or difficult, so we say yes when we really want to say no, or we let people overstep our limits because we don't want to upset them. But boundaries are not about shutting people out; they're about protecting your energy, time, and well-being so that you can live authentically and purposefully.

In this chapter, we will explore the importance of setting boundaries and how they help you reclaim your power. You'll learn why boundaries are essential for your mental, emotional, and spiritual health, and how to establish them with confidence and compassion. By the end of this chapter, you'll feel empowered to set healthy boundaries in your life without guilt or fear, knowing that boundaries are an act of love—for yourself and others.

Understanding the Purpose of Boundaries:

Many people misunderstand boundaries, thinking that they are about pushing people away or building walls. But in reality, boundaries are about creating a healthy space between you and others, where respect and understanding can flourish. They are not meant to isolate you but to protect your well-being, energy, and time so that you can live in alignment with your values.

Boundaries are like fences—they keep the good in and the bad out. They allow you to say "yes" to what aligns with your purpose and "no" to what drains or distracts you. When you set boundaries, you are essentially saying, "This is how I expect to be treated, and this is what I will and won't tolerate." Boundaries are not about controlling others; they are about controlling what you allow into your life.

God models boundaries for us in His Word. In Matthew 5:37, Jesus says, "Let your 'Yes' be 'Yes,' and your 'No,' 'No.'" This verse emphasizes the importance of clarity and integrity in our decisions and actions. When we set clear boundaries, we honor both our own needs and the needs of others, fostering healthier relationships and a stronger sense of self-respect.

Why We Struggle with Boundaries:
Despite the importance of boundaries, many of us find it difficult to set them. There are several reasons why we struggle with boundaries:

1. **Fear of Rejection:**
   One of the most common reasons we hesitate to set boundaries is the fear that others will reject us. We worry that if we say no, people will be upset with us, and we'll lose their approval or affection. This fear often stems from a deep desire to be liked and accepted. However, people who truly care about you will respect your boundaries. If someone rejects you because you set a healthy boundary, it says more about them than it does about you.

2. **Guilt and People-Pleasing:**
   Many of us have been conditioned to believe that saying no is selfish or unkind. We prioritize others' needs over our own, often to our own detriment. This people-pleasing mindset makes it difficult to set boundaries because we feel guilty for putting

ourselves first. But here's the truth: taking care of yourself is not selfish—it's necessary. You cannot serve others effectively if you are constantly drained or overwhelmed.

3. **Unclear Expectations:**
   Sometimes, we don't set boundaries because we're not clear about what our own needs and limits are. If you're unsure of what you want or need, it's challenging to communicate that to others. Taking the time to reflect on what matters most to you—whether it's your time, energy, emotional well-being, or values—will help you set clearer and more effective boundaries.

4. **Fear of Conflict:**
   Boundaries often require us to have difficult conversations, and many of us avoid confrontation at all costs. We worry that setting a boundary will create tension or conflict in our relationships, so we stay silent. However, avoiding conflict only leads to resentment and burnout. Boundaries, when communicated with love and respect, can actually strengthen relationships by fostering honesty and mutual respect.

5. **Low Self-Worth:**
   If you struggle with self-worth, you may feel that your needs and desires are not as important as others'. This belief makes it difficult to assert your boundaries because you don't feel entitled to them. But God has given you inherent worth, and you deserve to protect your well-being. Setting boundaries is an act of self-respect that acknowledges your value and affirms your right to be treated with kindness and dignity.

Biblical Foundations for Setting Boundaries:
Boundaries are not just a modern psychological concept—they are deeply rooted in Scripture. The Bible teaches us the importance of boundaries in our relationships, both with others and with ourselves. Consider these biblical principles related to boundaries:

- **Proverbs 4:23:** "Above all else, guard your heart, for everything you do flows from it."
  This verse reminds us that we are responsible for guarding our hearts, which means setting boundaries to protect our emotional and spiritual well-being. Boundaries allow us to be selective about what and who we let into our hearts.

- **Galatians 6:5:** "For each one should carry their own load."
  This scripture highlights personal responsibility. While we are called to help others, we are not meant to take on their burdens to the detriment of our own well-being. Setting boundaries helps us support others without becoming overwhelmed or depleted.

- **Matthew 14:23:** "After he had dismissed them, he went up on a mountainside by himself to pray."
  Even Jesus set boundaries. He often withdrew from the crowds to rest, pray, and reconnect with God. This shows us that it is not only okay but necessary to take time for ourselves, even when others demand our attention.

These scriptures affirm that boundaries are a God-given way to protect our well-being and ensure that we are living in alignment with His purpose for us. Boundaries help us honor the unique calling God has placed on our lives by making space for what truly matters.

The Benefits of Setting Boundaries:
Setting boundaries can feel uncomfortable at first, especially if you're not used to advocating for yourself. But the benefits of boundaries far outweigh the discomfort of setting them. Here are some of the key benefits of healthy boundaries:

1. **Increased Self-Respect:**
   Boundaries are an act of self-respect. When you set and uphold boundaries, you are affirming that your needs, time, and well-being are important. This helps build a stronger sense of self-worth and confidence.

2. **Healthier Relationships:**
   While it may seem counterintuitive, setting boundaries actually leads to healthier relationships. Boundaries create clarity and mutual respect, allowing both parties to understand and honor each other's needs. Relationships without boundaries often become codependent, resentful, or strained.

3. **Less Burnout and Overwhelm:**
   Without boundaries, we can easily overextend ourselves, saying yes to too many commitments and responsibilities. This leads to burnout, stress, and physical exhaustion. Boundaries help you prioritize what truly matters and protect your energy so that you can show up fully for the things and people that are most important to you.

4. **Emotional and Mental Health:**
   Setting boundaries is crucial for your emotional and mental well-being. Boundaries help you manage stress, protect your peace, and create space for self-care. When you set boundaries, you give yourself permission to take care of your emotional health without feeling guilty.

5. **Clarity and Focus:**
   Boundaries allow you to focus on what aligns with
   your values, goals, and purpose. When you're
   clear about your priorities, you can say no to
   distractions or obligations that pull you away from
   what's most important. This leads to greater
   clarity and focus in your life.

How to Set Boundaries with Confidence:

Setting boundaries can feel daunting, especially if
you're not used to asserting yourself. But with practice,
you can learn to set boundaries with confidence and
compassion. Here are some practical steps to help you
set boundaries effectively:

1. **Identify Your Needs and Limits:**
   Before you can set boundaries, you need to be
   clear about what your needs and limits are. Take
   time to reflect on the areas of your life where you
   feel drained, overwhelmed, or disrespected. These
   are often indicators that a boundary needs to be
   set. Ask yourself, "What do I need to protect my
   peace, time, and well-being?"

2. **Communicate Clearly and Directly:**
   When setting a boundary, it's important to be
   clear and direct in your communication. You don't
   need to apologize or over-explain your reasons.
   Simply state your boundary with kindness and
   firmness. For example, "I won't be able to take on
   any additional projects this month," or "I need
   some time to recharge, so I'll be unavailable this
   weekend."

3. **Be Prepared for Pushback:**
   Not everyone will respond positively to your
   boundaries, especially if they're used to you
   saying yes all the time. Some people may try to

push back, guilt-trip, or manipulate you into changing your mind. Stay firm in your boundary, and remember that you are not responsible for how others react. Their response is a reflection of their own issues, not your worth.

4. **Practice Saying No:**
   Saying no is one of the most important skills you can develop when setting boundaries. It can be uncomfortable at first, but the more you practice, the easier it becomes. Remember that saying no to something that drains you is saying yes to your well-being. You don't need to offer long explanations—simply saying, "No, I can't commit to that," is enough.

5. **Stay Consistent:**
   Boundaries only work if you consistently uphold them. If you set a boundary and then allow others to violate it, the boundary becomes meaningless. Stay consistent in enforcing your boundaries, even when it's difficult. Over time, people will learn to respect your limits, and you will feel more empowered in your relationships.

Boundaries in Relationships:

Setting boundaries in relationships can be one of the most challenging, yet rewarding, things you do. Whether it's with family, friends, or romantic partners, boundaries help create healthy, balanced relationships based on mutual respect.

In unhealthy relationships, boundaries may be blurred or nonexistent, leading to codependency, resentment, or manipulation. But when you establish boundaries, you protect both your well-being and the integrity of the relationship. Boundaries allow you to love others without losing yourself in the process.

Here are some key boundaries to consider in relationships:

- **Emotional Boundaries:** Protect your emotional well-being by recognizing when someone's behavior is harmful or manipulative. You have the right to distance yourself from negativity or toxicity.

- **Time Boundaries:** Be clear about how much time you're willing to spend with others, especially if you feel overwhelmed or drained by certain relationships. It's okay to take breaks or limit interactions when needed.

- **Physical Boundaries:** Respect your own personal space and comfort levels, and make sure others do the same. Physical boundaries are important in both romantic and platonic relationships.

- **Mental Boundaries:** Protect your peace by setting limits on conversations that stress or overwhelm you. It's okay to say, "I'm not comfortable discussing this topic right now," or "I need some time to process my thoughts."

Remember, boundaries are an act of love. When you set healthy boundaries, you are not only protecting yourself but also fostering healthier, more respectful relationships.

Boundaries with Yourself:

While boundaries with others are important, it's equally important to set boundaries with yourself. These are the boundaries that help you stay disciplined, focused, and aligned with your values. Without self-boundaries, it's easy to fall into patterns of procrastination, overindulgence, or neglect of your own well-being.

Here are some examples of self-boundaries:

- **Time Management:** Set limits on how much time you spend on distractions like social media, TV, or other activities that take away from your priorities.

- **Self-Care:** Make a commitment to prioritize your physical, emotional, and spiritual health by setting aside time for rest, exercise, and personal growth.

- **Financial Boundaries:** Establish limits on your spending to ensure that you're being responsible with your resources and not overspending on things that don't align with your values.

Setting boundaries with yourself requires self-discipline, but it also leads to greater peace and fulfillment. When you honor your own limits, you create a life that is aligned with your purpose and values.

Conclusion:

Setting boundaries is one of the most empowering things you can do for yourself. It allows you to reclaim your time, energy, and well-being while creating space for what truly matters in your life. Boundaries are not about keeping people out—they are about protecting your peace and honoring your worth.

As you begin to set boundaries in your life, remember that you are worthy of respect, love, and care. You don't need to apologize for protecting your well-being. Boundaries are an act of love, and they create the foundation for healthier, more fulfilling relationships.

Trust that by setting boundaries, you are living in alignment with God's purpose for your life. You are reclaiming your power and stepping into the fullness of who He created you to be.

Affirmations for Boundaries:

1. I have the right to set healthy boundaries in my life. My boundaries are a reflection of my self-worth and self-respect.

2. I protect my energy by saying no to what does not serve me.

3. I create space for relationships that uplift and support me.

4. My boundaries are acts of love for myself and others.

Reflections - Exercise #11:

1. Where in my life do I need to set stronger boundaries?

2. How has a lack of boundaries affected my energy and well-being?

3. What fears do I have around setting boundaries, and how can I overcome them?

4. How can setting boundaries create more peace and balance in my life?

Chapter 12: Trusting Divine Timing – Patience and Faith in the Waiting

Speak: Faith-centered and calming tone, focused on trust and patience

Introduction:

We live in a fast-paced world where instant gratification is the norm. From on-demand entertainment to same-day delivery, we're accustomed to getting what we want when we want it. But life, particularly a life rooted in faith, doesn't always operate on our timetable. We've all experienced moments when we've prayed, worked hard, or waited for a breakthrough, only to find that the answer didn't come as quickly as we had hoped. During these times of waiting, it's easy to grow frustrated, anxious, or even lose hope.

However, there is profound wisdom and growth to be found in the waiting. God's timing, often called *Divine Timing*, is perfect, even when it doesn't align with our expectations. Trusting in divine timing requires patience, faith, and the understanding that what is meant for you will not pass you by. It calls for the belief that God's plan is always better than our own, and that He knows the perfect moment to reveal His blessings.

In this chapter, we will explore the concept of trusting divine timing and the importance of patience in our spiritual journey. We will look at how to cultivate faith during seasons of waiting and how to embrace the process, knowing that every delay has a purpose. By the end of this chapter, you will see the waiting period not as a burden but as a time of preparation and growth.

Understanding Divine Timing:

Divine timing refers to the belief that everything

happens according to God's perfect plan and schedule. It's the idea that no matter how much we try to rush or control events in our lives, things will unfold exactly as they are meant to when the time is right. This can be a difficult concept to grasp, especially when we feel ready for something now, whether it's a new job, a relationship, or a long-awaited dream. But God's timing is based on His infinite wisdom and knowledge, and He sees the bigger picture that we often cannot.

One of the most powerful verses about divine timing is found in Ecclesiastes 3:1, which says, "There is a time for everything, and a season for every activity under the heavens." This verse reminds us that life unfolds in seasons, and each season has its own purpose. Just as there are times of growth and harvest, there are also times of rest and waiting. Understanding that life has seasons helps us to trust that even in the waiting, God is working.

Think of divine timing like the growth of a tree. A tree doesn't sprout overnight. First, the seed is planted, then it takes root beneath the surface, where no one can see. It needs time to grow strong roots before it can push through the soil and begin to bloom. The same is true for us. Sometimes, God is working beneath the surface of our lives, strengthening our roots and preparing us for what's to come. Just because we can't see the progress doesn't mean it's not happening.

The Importance of Patience in the Waiting:
Waiting is one of the most challenging aspects of life. We are often in a hurry to get to the next chapter, the next goal, or the next blessing. But patience is a crucial part of trusting God's timing. It's not just about sitting idly by and waiting for things to happen; it's about trusting that God is working, even when we don't see it.

In Psalm 27:14, we are encouraged to "Wait for the Lord; be strong and take heart and wait for the Lord." This verse reminds us that waiting requires strength and courage. It's not passive—it's an active decision to trust God in the process. Patience is not about inaction; it's about faith in action. It's about continuing to pray, work, and believe, even when the results aren't immediate.

In seasons of waiting, it's easy to become frustrated or impatient, wondering why things aren't happening as quickly as we'd like. We may start to question God's plan or even feel forgotten. But the truth is, God is never late, and He never forgets. His timing is always perfect because it aligns with His purpose for our lives. Patience allows us to trust that God is orchestrating things behind the scenes in ways we can't yet understand.

Learning to Trust God's Plan:
Trusting in divine timing requires trusting God's plan for your life. It means believing that He knows what is best for you, even when you feel like you know what's best. Proverbs 3:5-6 is a familiar verse that perfectly captures this idea: "Trust in the Lord with all your heart and lean not on your own understanding; in all your ways submit to him, and he will make your paths straight."

Often, we lean on our own understanding, thinking that we know the best path forward. But God's wisdom far exceeds our own. He sees what we cannot see and knows what we cannot know. When we trust His plan, we are surrendering our need to control the outcome and placing our faith in the One who holds the future.

Consider the story of Joseph in the Bible. As a young man, Joseph had dreams of greatness, but his life took a series of unexpected turns. He was sold into slavery by his brothers, falsely accused of a crime, and thrown into prison. For years, it seemed like Joseph's life was on hold, but all the while, God was working behind the scenes. Eventually, Joseph was elevated to a position of power in Egypt, and he was able to save many lives, including his own family. Joseph's story teaches us that even in the darkest times, God is working out His plan. What seemed like a series of setbacks were actually stepping stones to Joseph's purpose.

Trusting God's plan means believing that even when things don't make sense in the moment, God is aligning everything for your good. Romans 8:28 reminds us that "in all things God works for the good of those who love him, who have been called according to his purpose." Trust that the delay is not denial—it's preparation.

Embracing the Process of Waiting:
One of the hardest things to do in life is to embrace the process of waiting. We often want the result without the process, the blessing without the preparation. But just like a seed needs time to grow into a tree, we need time to grow into the person God has called us to be.

The process of waiting refines us. It teaches us patience, perseverance, and faith. It helps us grow spiritually, emotionally, and mentally so that when the blessing arrives, we are ready to receive it. The waiting season is often a season of preparation, where God is equipping us for what's to come.

Consider the Israelites' journey through the wilderness. After being freed from slavery in Egypt, they spent 40 years wandering in the desert before entering the Promised Land. The waiting wasn't a punishment—it was a time of preparation. God was teaching them to rely on Him, molding them into the people He had called them to be. Without the wilderness, they wouldn't have been ready for the Promised Land.

In your own life, waiting may feel frustrating or pointless, but it's never wasted. God is always at work, even when you can't see it. He's preparing you, strengthening you, and positioning you for what's ahead. Embrace the process, knowing that every step is part of His greater plan.

Surrendering Control:
One of the most challenging aspects of trusting divine timing is surrendering control. We want things to happen on our schedule, and we often try to force outcomes or rush the process. But control is an illusion. No matter how hard we try to manipulate circumstances, the truth is that we are not in control—God is.

Surrendering control doesn't mean giving up or doing nothing. It means letting go of the need to control every detail and trusting that God's timing is better than ours. It's about releasing the pressure to make things happen and resting in the assurance that God is orchestrating everything according to His perfect plan.

In Philippians 4:6-7, Paul writes, "Do not be anxious about anything, but in every situation, by prayer and petition, with thanksgiving, present your requests to God. And the peace of God, which transcends all understanding, will guard your hearts and your minds in Christ Jesus." This verse encourages us to bring our desires and concerns to God, but then to let go of the anxiety and trust Him with the outcome.

When you surrender control, you experience a sense of peace that comes from knowing that you are in God's hands. You no longer have to strive or stress because you trust that God is working everything out in His perfect timing. Surrender is not weakness—it's an act of faith.

The Power of Gratitude in the Waiting:

Gratitude is a powerful tool for maintaining peace and faith during seasons of waiting. When we focus on what we don't have or what hasn't happened yet, it's easy to become discouraged or impatient. But when we shift our focus to what we do have and the ways God has already blessed us, we begin to see the waiting as part of a larger story.

1 Thessalonians 5:18 says, "Give thanks in all circumstances; for this is God's will for you in Christ Jesus." This verse reminds us that gratitude isn't just for the good times—it's for every season, including the waiting season. Gratitude helps us shift our perspective from lack to abundance, from frustration to faith.

In moments of waiting, take time to reflect on the ways God has already been faithful in your life. What prayers has He answered? What blessings has He provided? What lessons have you learned? Gratitude grounds us in the present and reminds us that God's timing has always been perfect in the past, so we can trust Him with the future.

What to Do While You Wait:

Waiting doesn't mean doing nothing. While you wait for God's timing, there are things you can do to stay engaged and grow in your faith:

1. **Continue Praying:**
   Prayer is one of the most powerful ways to stay connected to God during the waiting season. Keep bringing your desires, concerns, and hopes to Him in prayer, and trust that He hears you. Even if the

answer doesn't come right away, know that God is working in ways you cannot see.

2. **Stay Active in Your Calling:**
   Don't put your life on hold while you wait for the next blessing. Continue to serve, work, and live out your calling, knowing that God will open the next door when the time is right. There is purpose in every season, even the waiting season.

3. **Cultivate Faith and Patience:**
   Use the waiting time to deepen your faith and develop patience. Trust that the waiting is growing your character and preparing you for what's ahead. James 1:4 says, "Let perseverance finish its work so that you may be mature and complete, not lacking anything." The waiting is refining you.

4. **Practice Gratitude:**
   Focus on the blessings in your life right now. Write down what you are thankful for and reflect on how God has been faithful to you in the past. Gratitude helps shift your focus from what's missing to what's present.

5. **Stay Connected to Community:**
   Don't isolate yourself during the waiting season. Stay connected to your community—whether that's friends, family, or a faith group. Surround yourself with people who will encourage you and remind you of God's faithfulness.

Conclusion:
Trusting divine timing is one of the most challenging, yet rewarding, aspects of faith. It requires patience, surrender, and a deep belief that God's plan is better than our own. While waiting can be difficult, it is not wasted time. God is using the waiting season to prepare

you, strengthen you, and align everything according to His perfect will.

As you wait for the next chapter to unfold, remember that God is working behind the scenes, even when you can't see it. Trust that His timing is perfect and that what is meant for you will not pass you by. Embrace the process, let go of the need for control, and rest in the assurance that God is always on time.

Affirmations for Trusting Divine Timing:

1. I trust God's timing for my life and my journey. What is meant for me will come at the right time.

2. I am patient and at peace, knowing that everything is unfolding in divine order.

3. I use this time of waiting to grow and prepare for what's to come.

4. God's plan is always better than mine, and I trust Him fully.

Reflections – Exercise #12:

1. Where in my life am I struggling to trust God's timing?

2. How can I embrace this season of waiting as a time of preparation?

3. What lessons is God teaching me during this period of waiting?

4. How can I cultivate more patience and faith in the process?

Chapter 13: Overcoming Fear of Failure – Finding Strength in God's Grace

Speak: Empowering and compassionate tone, focused on resilience and faith

Introduction:

Fear of failure is something that touches nearly everyone at some point in life. It's that nagging voice in the back of our minds that says, "What if I'm not good enough?" or "What if I try and fall short?" Fear of failure can paralyze us, keeping us from stepping into the opportunities and purpose that God has set before us. It holds us back from pursuing our dreams, deepening our relationships, and living the full, abundant life that God desires for us.

But here's the truth: failure is not the end. In fact, failure is a natural part of the growth process, and it is often through our failures that we learn, grow, and draw closer to God. Instead of viewing failure as something to fear, we can see it as an opportunity to experience God's grace, mercy, and strength in new ways. God's grace covers our mistakes, and His love never wavers, even when we stumble.

In this chapter, we'll explore how to overcome the fear of failure and embrace the lessons that come from falling short. We'll look at how to find strength in God's grace and how failure, rather than defining us, can shape us into who we are meant to be. By the end, you will see that failure is not something to avoid at all costs, but a stepping stone toward growth and transformation.

Understanding the Fear of Failure:

The fear of failure is deeply rooted in the human experience. It's a fear that often stems from our desire to be accepted, loved, and successful in the eyes of others. We fear failure because we believe it will confirm our worst thoughts about ourselves—that we're not good enough, smart enough, or capable enough. And in a world that values achievement and perfection, failure feels like a direct attack on our worth.

But failure is inevitable. No matter how much we try to avoid it, every person will face moments of failure. Whether it's in our careers, relationships, or personal goals, there will be times when we fall short of our expectations or the expectations of others. The key is not to avoid failure but to change how we respond to it.

In 2 Corinthians 12:9, the Apostle Paul reminds us of a profound truth: "But he said to me, 'My grace is sufficient for you, for my power is made perfect in weakness.'" God's power is revealed not through our perfection but through our weakness. When we face failure, we have the opportunity to lean into God's grace and discover a strength that goes beyond our human limitations. Failure becomes less about what we couldn't do and more about what God can do through us.

The Role of Failure in Growth:
Failure, while painful, plays an essential role in our growth and development. Without failure, we wouldn't have the opportunity to learn, adjust, and improve. Consider how a child learns to walk. They don't get it right the first time. They stumble, fall, and often cry in frustration. But each fall teaches them something new about balance, strength, and coordination. Eventually, with persistence and support, they learn to walk confidently.

The same is true in our own lives. Failure is not an indicator that we are incapable; it is an invitation to learn, adjust, and keep going. In Proverbs 24:16, we are reminded, "For though the righteous fall seven times, they rise again." This verse speaks to the resilience that God gives us. Failure is not about how many times we fall but about our willingness to rise again.

God often uses our failures to refine us. Through failure, we learn humility, perseverance, and reliance on Him. Failure strips away our pride and forces us to confront our limitations, reminding us that we need God's strength to succeed. It is in these moments of weakness that God does some of His most transformative work in our lives.

One of the most powerful examples of failure leading to growth is the story of Peter. Peter, one of Jesus's closest disciples, famously denied knowing Jesus three times on the night of His arrest. This failure was devastating for Peter, who had vowed to stand by Jesus no matter what. Yet, after His resurrection, Jesus restored Peter, offering him grace and commissioning him to lead the early church. Peter's failure did not disqualify him; rather, it prepared him for the mission that lay ahead. Through his failure, Peter learned about grace, forgiveness, and his deep need for God's strength.

Letting Go of Perfectionism:
One of the reasons we fear failure so much is because of perfectionism. Perfectionism tells us that we need to get everything right all the time, that mistakes are unacceptable, and that our worth is tied to our performance. But perfectionism is not only unrealistic—it's exhausting. It sets us up for disappointment because it leaves no room for grace or growth.

Perfectionism is often driven by a fear of judgment. We worry that if we fail, others will see us as less competent, less valuable, or less worthy. But God's view of us is not based on our performance. In fact, the Bible consistently reminds us that God's love is unconditional. Romans 5:8 says, "But God demonstrates his own love for us in this: While we were still sinners, Christ died for us." This means that even in our imperfections and failures, God's love for us remains steadfast.

Letting go of perfectionism means embracing the truth that we are loved by God, not because of what we do but because of who we are. It means allowing ourselves to make mistakes and learn from them without attaching our worth to the outcome. When we let go of perfectionism, we make room for God's grace to fill in the gaps where we fall short.

Redefining Success and Failure:
One of the ways to overcome the fear of failure is by redefining what success and failure mean to you. Too often, we define success based on external factors—how much money we make, how many accolades we receive, or how others perceive us. But true success, in God's eyes, is not about worldly achievement. It's about obedience, faithfulness, and growth.

Colossians 3:23 reminds us, "Whatever you do, work at it with all your heart, as working for the Lord, not for human masters." When we shift our focus from seeking approval from others to serving God with our whole hearts, our definition of success changes. Success becomes less about the outcome and more about the process—about whether we are living in alignment with God's will and purpose for our lives.

In the same way, failure is not the opposite of success—it's a part of the journey. Failure is not final, and it does not define who we are. Instead, it is an opportunity to grow, to refine our character, and to learn how to trust God more deeply. When we redefine success and failure through the lens of faith, we free ourselves from the pressure to be perfect and open ourselves to the lessons that God wants to teach us through both our successes and our failures.

Finding Strength in God's Grace:
One of the most beautiful aspects of our faith is that we don't have to rely solely on our own strength. God's grace is sufficient for every weakness, every mistake, and every failure. When we fail, God doesn't turn His back on us. Instead, He invites us to come to Him, to receive His grace, and to keep moving forward.

In Hebrews 4:16, we are encouraged to "approach God's throne of grace with confidence, so that we may receive mercy and find grace to help us in our time of need." This verse reminds us that when we fail, we can confidently come to God, knowing that He will meet us with grace and mercy. Failure doesn't disqualify us from God's love—it draws us closer to it.

When we find strength in God's grace, we no longer see failure as the end. Instead, we see it as a place of new beginnings, a place where God's power can work through our weaknesses. We realize that it's not about being perfect or never making mistakes—it's about relying on God's strength and trusting that He is working all things together for our good.

Overcoming Fear Through Faith:
Faith is the antidote to fear. When we place our trust in God, we are reminded that we are not in control—He is.

We may not know what the future holds or how things will turn out, but we can trust that God is with us every step of the way. In Isaiah 41:10, God says, "So do not fear, for I am with you; do not be dismayed, for I am your God. I will strengthen you and help you; I will uphold you with my righteous right hand."

Overcoming the fear of failure requires a shift in focus. Instead of focusing on what could go wrong, we focus on God's promises. We remember that He is faithful, that He will provide, and that His plans for us are good. When we live by faith rather than fear, we are free to take risks, try new things, and step into our purpose with boldness.

Faith doesn't mean that we won't ever fail, but it does mean that we are no longer defined by our failures. We are defined by God's love, grace, and calling on our lives. Fear of failure loses its power when we trust that even in our failures, God is at work, guiding us and shaping us for His purposes.

Practical Steps for Overcoming Fear of Failure:
Overcoming fear of failure is a process, but with faith and intentionality, you can begin to shift your mindset and approach life with greater confidence. Here are some practical steps to help you overcome the fear of failure:

1. **Acknowledge Your Fear:**
   The first step to overcoming fear is acknowledging it. Don't ignore or suppress your fear of failure—bring it to God in prayer. Ask Him to help you identify the root of your fear and to give you the courage to face it.

2. **Embrace Failure as Part of the Process:**
   Shift your mindset from seeing failure as something to avoid to seeing it as an opportunity

for growth. Remember that every failure teaches you something valuable and brings you closer to success. Celebrate your willingness to try, even if you don't get it right the first time.

3. **Redefine Success:**
Reflect on how you define success. Is it based on worldly standards or on your faith and values? Redefine success in a way that aligns with your faith—focus on obedience, faithfulness, and growth rather than external achievements.

4. **Rely on God's Grace:**
When you fail, turn to God for strength and grace. Remember that His love for you is not based on your performance but on who you are as His child. Trust that God's grace is sufficient to cover every mistake and that He will use even your failures for His glory.

5. **Take Action Despite Fear:**
Fear of failure can be paralyzing, but the best way to overcome it is to take action. Don't wait until you feel completely confident—step out in faith, knowing that God is with you. Each step you take will build your confidence and help you overcome the fear that holds you back.

Conclusion:
The fear of failure is a universal struggle, but it doesn't have to control your life. Failure is not the end—it's part of the journey toward growth, purpose, and deeper faith. When you trust in God's grace and lean on His strength, you can face failure with courage, knowing that it does not define you.

As you move forward, remember that failure is not something to be feared, but something to be embraced. It's a tool for learning, growth, and transformation. And through it all, God's grace is with you, guiding you and helping you rise again, no matter how many times you fall.

Affirmations for Overcoming Fear of Failure:

1. I am not defined by my failures; I am shaped by my resilience.

2. I embrace failure as part of my growth and trust in God's plan for my life.

3. I am worthy of love and success, regardless of past mistakes.

4. I trust God to turn my setbacks into opportunities for learning and growth.

5. I release the need for perfection and accept the beauty of progress.

Reflections – Exercise #13

1. Reflect on a time when you feared failure but chose to move forward anyway. How did God meet you in that situation?

2. What failures or mistakes from your past are still affecting you today? How can you invite God's grace into those areas for healing?

3. In what areas of your life are you holding back because of fear of failure? How might your life change if you stepped out in faith despite that fear?

4. Write about a failure that taught you an important lesson, and how did that experience help shape the person you are today?

5. How does the way you define success influence your fear of failure? What would change if you redefined success based on faithfulness rather than outcomes?

Chapter 14: Embracing Change – Navigating Life's Transitions with Courage and Faith

Speak: Empowering and compassionate tone, encouraging resilience and trust

Introduction:

Change is one of the few constants in life. Whether it's a new job, moving to a new place, the end of a relationship, or a shift in responsibilities, change can stir up a wide range of emotions—excitement, fear, uncertainty, and even resistance. While some of us welcome change, others dread it, seeing it as disruptive or unsettling. Regardless of how we feel about it, change is inevitable. But it is also an opportunity for growth, renewal, and stepping into new seasons of life.

The Bible is filled with stories of people who faced significant transitions—Abraham leaving his homeland, Moses leading the Israelites out of Egypt, and the disciples adjusting to life after Jesus's resurrection. In each case, God was with them, guiding them through the unknown and into His plan for their lives. Embracing change is not about avoiding uncertainty but about trusting that God is at work in every transition, using it to shape us and move us closer to His purpose for our lives.

In this chapter, we will explore how to navigate life's transitions with courage and faith. You will learn how to embrace change as an opportunity for growth, trust God in the process, and find peace in the midst of uncertainty. By the end of this chapter, you will be equipped with the tools to face change not with fear, but with confidence, knowing that God is in control.

Understanding the Nature of Change:

Change is an inevitable part of life. Seasons change, relationships evolve, careers shift, and we grow older.

Yet, even though change is natural, it can be difficult to navigate, especially when it feels like we're being pushed out of our comfort zone. We often resist change because it requires us to let go of what is familiar and step into the unknown.

One of the reasons change feels so uncomfortable is because it disrupts our sense of control. When things are stable and predictable, we feel secure. But when circumstances shift, we are forced to adapt, and that can be scary. But here's the truth: growth doesn't happen in comfort zones. Change, though uncomfortable, is a catalyst for personal and spiritual growth.

The Bible speaks to the natural rhythms of change in Ecclesiastes 3:1, which says, "There is a time for everything, and a season for every activity under the heavens." This verse reminds us that life unfolds in seasons, and each season has its purpose. Just as winter transitions into spring and night into day, our lives are filled with transitions that lead us from one phase to another. Instead of fearing these transitions, we can embrace them as part of God's design for our lives.

Why We Fear Change:
Fear of change is a common response, and it's rooted in several factors:

1. **Fear of the Unknown:**
   One of the biggest reasons we fear change is the uncertainty it brings. We don't know what's on the other side of the transition, and that uncertainty can make us anxious. Human beings are wired to seek security and stability, and when those are threatened, fear creeps in. We worry about whether we'll succeed, whether we'll be happy, or

whether we'll make the right decision. But while the future is uncertain to us, it is not uncertain to God. He knows the plans He has for us, and He promises to guide us through every transition.

2. **Loss of Control:**
Change often means we're no longer in control of the situation, and that can be unsettling. We like to plan our lives, but change can throw those plans into chaos. However, the need for control can lead to stress and frustration, especially when we realize that much of life is beyond our control. Trusting God means surrendering control and believing that He is sovereign over every aspect of our lives.

3. **Fear of Failure:**
With change comes the possibility of failure. Whether it's starting a new job or entering a new phase of life, the fear of not measuring up can hold us back. We wonder, "What if I fail? What if I'm not good enough?" But failure is not the end— it's often a necessary part of growth. God doesn't expect perfection from us, but He does call us to step out in faith, trusting that even if we stumble, He will guide us.

4. **Attachment to the Past:**
Sometimes, we resist change because we're attached to the way things used to be. We may feel nostalgic for a past season of life, whether it's a job, a relationship, or a particular routine. But holding on to the past can keep us from embracing the future. Philippians 3:13-14 encourages us to "forget what is behind and strain toward what is ahead." Letting go of the past doesn't mean forgetting it—it means releasing it so that we can fully embrace the new season God is leading us into.

5. **Fear of Losing Identity:**
   Change can sometimes make us question who we
   are. If we've tied our identity to a particular role,
   job, or relationship, a shift in those areas can
   leave us feeling lost. But our identity is not rooted
   in our circumstances—it's rooted in Christ. No
   matter how much our external world changes,
   who we are in God's eyes remains constant. We
   are His beloved children, and that identity never
   changes, even when everything else does.

Trusting God in the Midst of Change:

The key to navigating change with peace and
confidence is trusting that God is in control. Psalm
37:23 says, "The Lord makes firm the steps of the one
who delights in him." This verse reminds us that God is
not only aware of the changes in our lives—He is
actively guiding us through them. Even when we feel
like everything is shifting, God's presence is our
constant.

Trusting God in the midst of change doesn't mean we
won't feel fear or uncertainty. It means choosing to lean
into God's promises rather than our fears. It means
reminding ourselves that while we may not know what
the future holds, we know who holds the future.

Jeremiah 29:11 is a familiar verse that offers comfort
during times of transition: "For I know the plans I have
for you, declares the Lord, plans to prosper you and not
to harm you, plans to give you hope and a future." This
verse reassures us that God's plans are always good,
even when we don't fully understand them. Change is
often part of God's plan to bring us into a deeper
relationship with Him and to lead us toward the purpose
He has for our lives.

Embracing Change as a Path to Growth:
Change is not only inevitable—it is necessary for growth. Just as a seed must break through the ground to become a tree, we must go through transitions to become the people God has called us to be. Each change, whether big or small, presents an opportunity for personal, emotional, and spiritual growth.

Consider the story of Abraham. In Genesis 12:1, God called Abraham to leave his country, his people, and his father's household and go to a land that God would show him. Abraham had to leave behind everything familiar and comfortable, trusting that God had a plan for his life. Abraham's obedience to God's call led to the fulfillment of God's promise to make him the father of many nations. His willingness to embrace change was a key part of his spiritual journey.

Like Abraham, we are often called to step out of our comfort zones and into the unknown. Change pushes us to rely on God in ways we might not have when things were stable. It stretches our faith, deepens our trust, and refines our character. When we embrace change as a path to growth, we shift our perspective from fear to anticipation, knowing that God is using every transition to mold us into who He created us to be.

Practical Steps for Navigating Change with Courage and Faith:
Navigating change doesn't have to be overwhelming. With the right mindset and tools, you can move through transitions with confidence, trusting that God is with you every step of the way. Here are some practical steps to help you embrace change:

1. **Acknowledge Your Feelings:**
   Change can bring up a wide range of emotions—fear, excitement, sadness, or even anger. It's

important to acknowledge these feelings rather than suppress them. Take time to process how you're feeling about the transition, and bring those feelings to God in prayer. Remember, it's okay to feel uncertain or afraid, but don't let those emotions keep you from moving forward.

2. **Seek God's Guidance:**
   Before making any major decisions during a time of change, seek God's guidance through prayer. Ask Him for wisdom, clarity, and peace as you navigate the transition. James 1:5 reminds us, "If any of you lacks wisdom, you should ask God, who gives generously to all without finding fault, and it will be given to you." Trust that God will guide you as you seek Him.

3. **Stay Grounded in God's Word:**
   During times of change, it's important to stay rooted in Scripture. God's Word offers comfort, guidance, and encouragement when life feels uncertain. Make it a priority to spend time reading the Bible, meditating on God's promises, and reminding yourself of His faithfulness.

4. **Take One Step at a Time:**
   Change can feel overwhelming when we try to think too far ahead. Instead of focusing on the entire journey, focus on taking one step at a time. Trust that God will reveal the next step when the time is right. Proverbs 16:9 says, "In their hearts humans plan their course, but the Lord establishes their steps." Allow God to lead you one step at a time, knowing that He is guiding your path.

5. **Surround Yourself with Support:**
   Don't navigate change alone. Surround yourself with a supportive community of friends, family, or

faith-based groups who can encourage and pray for you during this season. Having people to lean on can make a big difference as you move through transitions.

Finding Peace in Uncertainty:
One of the hardest aspects of change is the uncertainty it brings. We want to know how things will turn out, but life rarely gives us that kind of certainty. However, peace is not found in having all the answers—it's found in trusting God. Philippians 4:6-7 offers us this powerful promise: "Do not be anxious about anything, but in every situation, by prayer and petition, with thanksgiving, present your requests to God. And the peace of God, which transcends all understanding, will guard your hearts and your minds in Christ Jesus."

God's peace is available to us even when we don't know what the future holds. When we surrender our anxieties and uncertainties to Him, He fills us with a peace that goes beyond our understanding. This peace allows us to move forward in faith, trusting that God is in control, even when the path ahead is unclear.

Letting Go of What No Longer Serves You:
In order to fully embrace change, we must be willing to let go of what no longer serves us. This could be an old mindset, a toxic relationship, a job that no longer aligns with our values, or even a version of ourselves that we've outgrown. Letting go can be difficult, especially when we're attached to what is familiar. But holding on to the past can prevent us from stepping into the future God has for us.

Isaiah 43:18-19 encourages us, "Forget the former things; do not dwell on the past. See, I am doing a new thing! Now it springs up; do you not perceive it?" God is always at work, doing new things in our lives. But we can't receive the new if we're still clinging to the old. Letting go is not about forgetting the past—it's about making space for the new blessings and opportunities that God is bringing into your life.

Conclusion:
Change is inevitable, but it doesn't have to be something we fear. With God's guidance, we can navigate life's transitions with courage, faith, and peace. Each change, whether expected or unexpected, is an opportunity to grow, trust God more deeply, and step into new seasons of life with confidence.

As you embrace the changes in your life, remember that you are not alone. God is with you, guiding your steps, providing for your needs, and offering you peace in the midst of uncertainty. Trust that He is working all things together for your good and that every change, no matter how difficult, is part of His perfect plan for your life.

Affirmations for Embracing Change:

1. Change is an opportunity for growth, and I embrace it with courage.

2. I am not defined by the past; I am stepping into the new season God has for me.

3. Each transition is preparing me for something greater, and I am ready to receive it.

4. I embrace the unknown with faith, knowing that God's promises are unchanging.

5. I let go of what no longer serves me and make space for new blessings in my life.

Reflections – Exercise #14:

1. What changes are you currently facing, and how are they making you feel? How can you invite God into this process?

2. Write about a time when you resisted change. What was the outcome, and what did you learn from the experience?

3. How do you typically respond to change? What steps can you take to embrace change with greater faith and trust in God?

4. What are some areas of your life where you need to let go of the past to fully embrace the future God has for you?

5. Reflect on a time when change brought unexpected blessings into your life. How did God use that transition to grow you?

____

____

____

____

____

____

____

____

____

Chapter 15: Building Resilience – Strengthening Your Faith in the Face of Adversity

Speak: Bold and encouraging tone, focused on perseverance and spiritual endurance

Introduction:

Life is filled with challenges—financial struggles, health crises, relationship difficulties, and moments of deep personal pain. We all encounter adversity at some point, and how we respond to it can shape the course of our lives. While adversity is inevitable, it's also an opportunity to build resilience, to strengthen our faith, and to grow in ways we never thought possible.

Resilience is the ability to bounce back from hardship, not by avoiding it but by facing it head-on and trusting that God is working through it. It's about standing firm in the storms of life, knowing that you are rooted in a faith that cannot be shaken. The Bible is filled with stories of men and women who endured great trials but emerged stronger because of their unwavering faith in God. In those stories, we see that resilience is not about being immune to pain but about having the strength to persevere, knowing that God is our refuge and strength.

In this chapter, we will explore how to build resilience in the face of adversity. We'll look at the role of faith, the power of perseverance, and the importance of hope when life feels overwhelming. By the end, you will feel empowered to stand strong in the midst of challenges, knowing that your resilience is rooted in God's promises.

Understanding Resilience:

Resilience doesn't mean that you won't face difficulties or that you'll never feel discouraged. Rather, it's about how you respond when adversity comes. It's the ability to maintain hope, faith, and courage in the face of obstacles, to get back up when you fall, and to continue moving forward even when life feels hard.

Psalm 46:1 reminds us, "God is our refuge and strength, an ever-present help in trouble." This verse is a powerful reminder that resilience is not something we muster up on our own. Our resilience comes from our relationship with God, who is our source of strength. When we are rooted in Him, we can face life's trials with confidence, knowing that we are never alone.

Resilience is not about being tough or emotionally detached. It's about having a deep trust in God's ability to carry you through adversity. It's about allowing yourself to grieve, process, and heal, but also finding the strength to keep going, knowing that God is with you every step of the way.

Why Adversity Is Part of the Journey:
Adversity is an inevitable part of life. No one is immune to hardship, and the Bible is clear that trials will come. In John 16:33, Jesus says, "In this world you will have trouble. But take heart! I have overcome the world." This verse is both a warning and a promise. Jesus doesn't sugarcoat the reality of life's difficulties, but He also offers the assurance that He has already overcome every challenge we will face.

So why does God allow adversity in our lives? While we may not always understand the specific reasons for our trials, we can trust that God uses adversity to shape and refine us. James 1:2-4 says, "Consider it pure joy, my brothers and sisters, whenever you face trials of many kinds, because you know that the testing of your faith produces perseverance. Let perseverance finish its work so that you may be mature and complete, not lacking anything." This passage teaches us that adversity is not a punishment—it's an opportunity for growth.

Through adversity, God refines our character, deepens our faith, and helps us develop the resilience needed to fulfill our purpose. Just as gold is refined in the fire, our faith is strengthened through the trials we face. Each challenge we encounter is an opportunity to rely more deeply on God, to grow in perseverance, and to become more like Christ.

Resilience Rooted in Faith:
Faith is the foundation of resilience. When we face challenges, it's easy to feel overwhelmed or defeated, but faith gives us the strength to keep going. Hebrews 11:1 defines faith as "confidence in what we hope for and assurance about what we do not see." Faith allows us to trust that God is working, even when we can't see the full picture.

When we are rooted in faith, we view adversity through a different lens. Instead of seeing hardship as a dead end, we see it as part of the journey—a journey that God is guiding every step of the way. Faith gives us the courage to keep moving forward, knowing that God is with us and that He will bring good out of even the most difficult situations.

One of the most powerful examples of resilience rooted in faith is the story of Job. Job was a man who lost everything—his wealth, his health, and his family. Yet, despite his immense suffering, Job never lost his faith in God. In Job 1:21, after losing his children and all his possessions, Job says, "The Lord gave and the Lord has taken away; may the name of the Lord be praised." Job's resilience came from his deep trust in God's sovereignty, even when he didn't understand why he was suffering.

Like Job, our resilience is strengthened when we trust that God is in control, even in the midst of adversity. We may not always understand why we are facing a particular challenge, but we can rest in the assurance that God is working all things for our good (Romans 8:28).

Perseverance in the Face of Challenges:

Perseverance is a key aspect of resilience. It's the ability to keep going, even when the road is hard and the outcome is uncertain. In Romans 5:3-4, Paul writes, "Not only so, but we also glory in our sufferings, because we know that suffering produces perseverance; perseverance, character; and character, hope." This verse reminds us that perseverance leads to growth—it strengthens our character and deepens our hope.

Perseverance is not about pretending that everything is fine or ignoring the pain of adversity. It's about choosing to move forward despite the difficulty. It's about trusting that God is with you, giving you the strength to take the next step, even when you feel like giving up.

Consider the story of the Israelites as they wandered in the wilderness for 40 years. They faced countless challenges—hunger, thirst, and uncertainty about their future. Yet, God was with them every step of the way, providing manna from heaven, water from rocks, and guidance through the cloud by day and the fire by night. Their journey required perseverance, and it was through that perseverance that they were ultimately prepared to enter the Promised Land.

Perseverance doesn't mean the journey will be easy, but it does mean that the journey is worth it. As we persevere through adversity, we become stronger, wiser, and more deeply connected to God's purpose for our lives.

The Power of Hope:

Hope is an essential part of resilience. It's the belief that no matter how difficult the present moment is, there is a brighter future ahead. Hope is what keeps us going when we feel like giving up. It reminds us that our story is not over and that God is still writing new chapters.

In Lamentations 3:22-23, we are reminded of the unending hope we have in God: "Because of the Lord's great love we are not consumed, for his compassions never fail. They are new every morning; great is your faithfulness." Even in the darkest moments, God's mercy is new every day, and His faithfulness never wavers. Hope allows us to trust that better days are coming, even when we can't yet see them.

Hope is not wishful thinking—it's a confident expectation rooted in God's promises. In times of adversity, hope gives us the strength to keep moving forward, believing that God will bring us through the storm. Psalm 27:13 says, "I remain confident of this: I will see the goodness of the Lord in the land of the living." This verse reminds us that God's goodness is not just for eternity—it's for here and now. Even in the midst of trials, we can have hope that we will experience God's goodness in our lives.

Practical Ways to Build Resilience:

Building resilience is a process that requires intentionality, faith, and perseverance. Here are some practical ways to strengthen your resilience in the face of adversity:

1. **Stay Connected to God in Prayer:**
   Prayer is your lifeline in times of adversity. When you feel overwhelmed, bring your fears, frustrations, and worries to God in prayer. Philippians 4:6-7 encourages us, "Do not be anxious about anything, but in every situation, by prayer and petition, with thanksgiving, present your requests to God. And the peace of God, which transcends all understanding, will guard your hearts and your minds in Christ Jesus." Through prayer, we receive peace, strength, and guidance from God.

2. **Surround Yourself with a Supportive Community:**
   Resilience is not something you have to build on your own. Surround yourself with a community of believers who can encourage, pray for, and support you during difficult times. Galatians 6:2 reminds us to "carry each other's burdens, and in this way you will fulfill the law of Christ." Having people who will walk with you through adversity can make a huge difference in how you navigate challenges.

3. **Focus on What You Can Control:**
   Adversity often brings a sense of powerlessness, but it's important to focus on what you can control, rather than what you can't. You may not be able to change your circumstances, but you can control how you respond to them. Focus on maintaining your faith, your mindset, and your actions, knowing that God is in control of the bigger picture.

4. **Keep a Gratitude Journal:**
   Gratitude is a powerful way to build resilience. When you focus on the blessings in your life, even in the midst of hardship, you shift your

perspective from lack to abundance. Start a gratitude journal and write down three things you are thankful for each day. This practice helps you stay grounded in God's goodness and reminds you of His faithfulness.

5. **Trust God's Timing:**
   Sometimes, adversity lasts longer than we'd like, and we wonder when it will end. Trust that God's timing is perfect, even when it doesn't align with your own. Isaiah 40:31 encourages us, "But those who hope in the Lord will renew their strength. They will soar on wings like eagles; they will run and not grow weary, they will walk and not be faint." Trust that God is working in your life, even when the road feels long.

Finding Purpose in Adversity:
One of the most powerful aspects of resilience is the ability to find purpose in adversity. God never wastes a trial—He uses every challenge to refine us and to accomplish His purposes in our lives. Romans 5:3-4 reminds us that suffering produces perseverance, character, and hope. Each trial we face is an opportunity to grow in these areas and to become more like Christ.

Consider the story of Joseph in the Old Testament. Joseph faced tremendous adversity—he was sold into slavery by his brothers, falsely accused, and thrown into prison. Yet, through it all, Joseph remained faithful to God, and in the end, he was elevated to a position of power where he was able to save many lives, including the lives of his brothers who had wronged him. In Genesis 50:20, Joseph says to his brothers, "You intended to harm me, but God intended it for good to accomplish what is now being done, the saving of many lives." Joseph's story reminds us that God can bring good out of even the most difficult circumstances.

When you face adversity, ask God to show you the purpose in your trial. Trust that He is using it to shape you, to strengthen you, and to prepare you for the next chapter of your life.

Conclusion:

Resilience is not about avoiding adversity—it's about standing strong in the face of it, knowing that God is with you every step of the way. Through faith, perseverance, and hope, you can overcome any challenge, not by your own strength but by relying on God's strength.

As you navigate the trials of life, remember that God is your refuge and strength, an ever-present help in trouble. He is refining you, shaping you, and preparing you for the good things He has planned for your future. With God's help, you can build the resilience needed to face life's challenges with courage, faith, and hope.

Affirmations for Building Resilience:

1. I am strong, resilient, and able to overcome any challenge with God's help. God is my refuge and strength, a very present help in times of trouble.

2. Each trial I face is shaping me into the person God created me to be. I can persevere because I know that God is with me every step of the way.

3. My hope is anchored in God's promises, and I trust that better days are coming. I have the strength to rise again, no matter how many times I fall.

4. God is using every challenge in my life to build my character and strengthen my faith. I choose faith over fear and trust that God's purpose is greater than my pain.

5. I remain confident that I will see God's goodness, even in the midst of adversity.

Reflections – Exercise #15:

1. Reflect on a difficult time in your life when you found strength in God. How did He help you persevere through that challenge?

2. What does resilience mean to you? How can you rely on your faith to build greater resilience in the face of current or future challenges?

3. Write about a time when you felt like giving up but chose to keep going. What gave you the strength to persevere?

4. What are some practical ways you can deepen your faith during times of adversity?

5. How can you cultivate hope, even when circumstances feel overwhelming or uncertain?

Summary

In this book, we've explored key themes that help you navigate the complexities of life with greater faith, resilience, and courage. Through each chapter, you have been given tools and wisdom to:

- **Overcome Fear of Failure**: You've learned to shift your perspective on failure, viewing it as a stepping stone toward growth rather than a defining setback. Through God's grace, you've discovered the strength to move forward with confidence, knowing that every mistake is an opportunity for learning and transformation.

- **Embrace Change**: Life's transitions, though challenging, are essential for personal and spiritual growth. You now understand that change is not something to fear but a divine process that draws you closer to God's plan for your life. You've learned how to release the past and open yourself to new opportunities with courage and faith.

- **Build Resilience**: Adversity is inevitable, but it is through trials that your character is strengthened. You've explored the power of perseverance and hope, and you've come to see that resilience is not about avoiding hardship but about rising stronger each time, with God as your refuge and strength.

- **Trust Divine Timing**: Patience is key in a world where instant results are often desired. You've come to trust that God's timing is perfect, even when the waiting feels difficult. Through faith, you've developed the ability to trust the process, knowing that what God has planned for you is always greater than anything you could have orchestrated yourself.

This book has been designed to not only uplift and inspire you but to also offer practical ways to apply these lessons to your daily life. With each chapter, you've been encouraged to reflect on your own experiences, pray through challenges, and cultivate habits that strengthen your faith and character.

The affirmations and journal prompts provided throughout are tools to help you continue on your journey of growth and transformation long after this book is finished. I encourage you to revisit these exercises whenever you need encouragement or a reminder of the strength that lies within you.

As you move forward, remember that no matter what challenges or changes you face, God is always with you—guiding you, sustaining you, and empowering you to live out your highest potential. You are stronger than you know, more capable than you realize, and deeply loved by the Creator of the universe. May you continue to walk boldly in faith, knowing that every step you take is part of God's divine plan for your life.

Thank you for allowing me to be part of your journey. I pray that you carry the lessons learned here into every aspect of your life and that you continue to grow in resilience, faith, and purpose. Be encouraged—your best days are still ahead.

Disclaimer:

The content of this book is intended for **inspirational and motivational purposes only**. While it is designed to encourage personal growth, spiritual development, and emotional well-being, it is not a substitute for professional mental health or medical advice, diagnosis, or treatment.

If you are experiencing physical or mental health concerns, we strongly encourage you to seek help from a qualified healthcare professional, counselor, or therapist. This book is meant to offer encouragement and support, but it does not replace the expertise of licensed professionals who can provide individualized care.

Always consult a healthcare provider before making any changes to your health or wellness routine, and reach out for professional support if you feel overwhelmed or are dealing with persistent emotional, psychological, or physical challenges.

By engaging with this book, you acknowledge that the author is not providing medical, psychological, or therapeutic services, and that any decisions or actions you take based on the content are your sole responsibility.

About the Author:

Cynthia Wade is an international Consultant, Trainer, and Speaker with over 30 years of expertise in IT and application development. Her extensive experience spans computer systems, business management, and education, making her a sought-after leader in the tech industry.

As a **serial entrepreneur** and **lifelong learner**, Cynthia is dedicated to empowering both new and seasoned entrepreneurs to embrace technology with confidence. Her teaching style breaks down complex technical concepts, making them accessible and easy to understand, so that individuals can thrive in today's fast-paced digital landscape.

Though now retired, Cynthia continues to share her wealth of knowledge through **speaking engagements** and **private training sessions**, staying at the forefront of the latest tech trends and innovations. Her mission is to help others harness the power of technology, enabling them to excel in their personal and professional endeavors.

MOTTO: "Stay Curious, Stay Inspired, Keep Learning."

Stay connected with Cynthia on social media:

- **Instagram**: @cwade214
- **Pinterest**: cafeimedia
- **Facebook**: cwade214

Explore Cynthia's work and projects:

- **Website**: ondemand.cierratec.net
- **Website**: www.cafeimedia.net
- **Shop**: cafeimedia.etsy.com